J. H. PLUMB

The First Four Georges

ENGLAND AND HER GERMAN KINGS

LITTLE, BROWN AND COMPANY · BOSTON · TORONTO

For Sydney Grose

CONTENTS

Preface   *page* 9

Acknowledgments   11

  I   *The Georgian World*   13

  II *George I, 1714-1727*   37

  III *George II, 1727-1760*   68

  IV *George III, 1760-1820*   96

  V   *George IV, Regent and King, 1812-1830*   148

Bibliography   178

Index   183

ILLUSTRATIONS

between pages 96–7

"The Second Stage of Cruelty"—a London street of 1715

George I, *from a five-guinea piece*

George II, *from a five-guinea piece*

George III, *from a gold guinea*

George IV, *from a gold sovereign*

George I,
  from a contemporary portrait by an unknown artist

George II,
  from the portrait by F. Worlidge

George II,
  from the bust by Louis François Roubillac

Caroline of Anspach, *from the bust by J. M. Rysbrack*

Frederick Prince of Wales and his Sisters,
  from the painting by J. F. Nollekens

George III, in his Coronation robes,
  from the portrait painted in the studio of Allan Ramsay

Charlotte of Mecklenburg-Strelitz,
  from the painting by Peter Edward Stroehling

George III,
  from the portrait by Thomas Gainsborough

George IV,
  from the portrait by Sir Thomas Lawrence

Caroline of Brunswick,
  from the portrait by Samuel Lane

Mrs. Fitzherbert,
  from the portrait by Thomas Gainsborough

George IV in Highland dress,
 from the portrait by Sir David Wilkie
Caroline of Brunswick,
 from a Wedgwood medallion
George IV as Prince of Wales,
 from a Wedgwood medallion
George IV, when Prince of Wales,
 from the painting by George Stubbs

PREFACE

The first four Georges have not enjoyed a good press since Thackeray's day. The first two are usually dismissed as stupid and quite uninterested in things English—a stroke of fortune which permitted cabinet government and the two-party system to flourish unhampered. The third, glorying in the name of Briton, tried to ape the Stuarts, and in so doing, lost the American colonies. Fortunately, insanity and Pitt restored the balance of the constitution. The public life of George IV is usually ignored and attention focused on the elegance of his furnishings. Poor creatures, they have all been judged by standards which were not their own nor their contemporaries. Just how true or false these judgements are will be seen in the following pages, in which I have attempted to portray the Georges as human beings caught in exceptional circumstances.

It is almost impossible for a monarch to be dull, no matter how stupid. The exceptional opportunities for the untrammelled development of personal attitudes act like a powerful fertiliser on the human temperament. And the Georges, who in ordinary circumstances would have been commonplace men, become a little larger than life and impress their personalities on the course of English history.

During their epoch the long struggle between the Crown and Parliament was resolved by the curious development of a parliamentary monarchy. Kings were still expected to rule as well as reign, but to subject their financial arrangements, and by implication their foreign policy, to the judgement of a House of Commons; a body, however, which was representative only of the very wealthiest classes. Nevertheless, from 1714-1830, the monarchy was the mainspring of political life, and the character and abilities of the Georges were of great consequence in the destinies of their nation—a situation of which each one of them was acutely aware. Not one of them was a cipher. All, including George I, were passionately interested in their rights, powers, and privileges as Kings of Great Britain.

I have been greatly privileged in being graciously permitted to consult certain documents in the Royal Archives at Windsor. I am also indebted to Mr. R. W. Ketton-Cremer and the Trustees of the Chatsworth Settlement for either drawing my attention to documents or for permission to quote from them. I wish to acknowledge, too, the kindness of Mr. Roger Fulford and Messrs Duckworth for permission to quote from his excellent book on George IV, and also of Professor Alden and Messrs Hamish Hamilton for permission to quote from *The American Revolution*.

J. H. PLUMB

ACKNOWLEDGMENTS

The picture of George II from the bust by Louis François Roubillac, the picture of Caroline of Anspach from the bust by J. M. Rysbrack, the painting of Frederick Prince of Wales and his Sisters by J. F. Nollekens, the portrait of Charlotte of Mecklenburg-Strelitz, the portrait of George III by Thomas Gainsborough, and the portraits of George IV by Sir Thomas Lawrence and George Stubbs are reproduced by Gracious Permission of Her Majesty The Queen.

The Author and Publishers wish to thank the following for permission to reproduce the illustrations in this book:

The Ashmolean Museum (by courtesy of Dr. C. H. V. Sutherland), for the pictures of the gold guinea of George III and the gold sovereign of George IV; A. H. Baldwin & Sons Ltd., for the pictures of the five-guinea pieces of George I and George II; Cailfornia Palace of the Legion of Honour, for the portrait of Mrs. Fitzherbert by Thomas Gainsborough; The Marquess of Cholmondeley, for the portrait of George I by an unknown artist; The National Galleries of Scotland, for the portrait of Caroline of Brunswick by Samuel Lane; The National Portrait Gallery for, the portraits of George II by F. Worlidge and George III, in his Coronation Robes; The Royal Academy of Arts, for the bust of George II by Louis François Roubillac; The Wedgwood Museum, for the pictures of the Wedgwood medallions of Caroline of Brunswick and George IV as Prince of Wales; The Wellington Museum, Apsley House, London, for the portrait of George IV in Highland dress by Sir David Wilkie.

CHAPTER I

THE GEORGIAN WORLD

The physical remains of the age of the Georges are almost uniformly of an elegance of design rarely achieved since. Palaces by Kent or Adam, terrace houses by Wood, print by Baskerville, china by Wedgwood, the bridges and aqueducts of Brindley's canals; tea-caddies, snuff-boxes, bird cages, and doll's furniture; in all, the design is controlled by an instinctive sense of proportion. The same preoccupation runs through much of the poetry and the prose, the painting and the music of the time. This basic uniformity of Georgian style is easily recognisable, and this in its turn has created the idea of an age which agrees but little with its reality. It is true that the physical world of the eighteenth century was, for the wealthy classes, as elegant as the innumerable conversation pieces have depicted it. Pictures of young men, immaculate in silk and satin, toying with a delicate china tea-cup, leaning forward with studied, careless charm to talk to young women as beautifully dressed as themselves, are neither false nor sentimental. The splendid clothes, the delicate furniture, the superb formal backgrounds of building and landscape are real enough. What is unreal are the ideas to which such pictures give rise. They create a sense of calm urbanity, of restrained good breeding, a little heartless, perhaps, and rather artificial. The world in which these creatures moved seems incompatible with violence and aggression, with coarse language and gross manners, with dirt, disease and lust. It is hard to believe that Gainsborough's diaphanous creatures, gliding with such grace in the freshness of the morning, were of an earthiness both in speech and in action that would shock what we like to think of as a franker age. Alongside Gainsborough, Reynolds, Zoffany or Stubbs must be placed the savage pictures of Hogarth and the brutal squibs of Rowlandson and Gillray. Although caricature plays an undeniable part in their composition, the world which they depict is closer to the historical records of Georgian society; far closer than the pictures of the fashionable world.

Perhaps the most obvious but least recognised feature of English life in the eighteenth and early nineteenth century was its love of aggression. Rarely has the world known a more aggressive society, or one in which passion was more openly or violently expressed. This may seem paradoxical, for in no other age was enthusiasm so constantly deplored. Enthusiasm was related, however, to intellectual or moral fervour, not animal spirits; high animal spirits and a frank indulgence of them were the keynotes to this age. There are few beasts, and man not one of them, which do not relish barking, biting and fighting. To vast numbers of eighteenth-century Englishmen wars were welcome; golden opportunities to beggar their neighbours, to seize the wealth of the world and to demonstrate the contempt in which the nation held those Pope-ridden, frog-eating, puny, wooden-shoed slaves, the French. Fame was accorded to the rashest of heroes—Clive at Arcot, Wolfe at Quebec, Nelson at Aboukir; disgrace and death on the quarter-deck was Byng's lot for allowing caution and wisdom to prevail. The manic fury of Chatham's denunciations suited the Englishman's mood. The endless stream of clamorous abuse which poured from the press both stimulated and satisfied the same yearning for violence.

No nation rioted more easily or more savagely—from 1714 to 1830 angry mobs, burning and looting, were as prevalent as disease, and as frequent in the countryside as in the great towns. Time and time again the gentry were forced to assemble and put down the rioting workmen by force. In 1756 the high price of corn brought out the Shropshire colliers. " The mob gave themselves the title of Levelers," wrote Hannah Darby, an eye-witness, " and so they were indeed—this night the gentlemen muster'd up several hundred men, to suppress them, they were all arm'd and marched up our railway. They made a formidable appearance; they met with the mob at Ketley and they stood three fires before they fled."[1] Gloucestershire was so riotous in 1734 that the army was needed to restore order: Suffolk, later in the century, suffered a miniature civil war. For a few days in June 1780 London and Southwark were at the mercy of the mob—Horace Walpole, who had lived through " the Excise and the Gin Act, and the rebels at Derby, and Wilkes's interlude ", had never witnessed anything comparable. Mobs and destruction—they were a part of life, an expression of those sharp conflicts in society which helped to foster the spirit of the nation. Riots and rebellions were not confined to the lower orders; schoolboys knew how to do battle. Winchester enjoyed three sharp mutinies between 1766 and 1793; Wellesley was removed from Harrow in 1771 after a large-scale riot; the imprisoning and beating of masters, breaking of furniture, or an emphatic refusal to work, were commonplaces of school life, and as much a part of it as the remorseless floggings and the endless bullying of smaller boys.

The amusements of all classes were streaked with blood

[1] A. Raistrick, *A Dynasty of Ironfounders*, 78-9.

and cruelty. Cock-fighting and bear- and bull-baiting were little more than shambles; prize-fighting was carried on in the savagest manner; blood sports were popular and wide-spread—more popular and more widespread than many care to believe, and some containing far more blood than sport. Goose-riding was a well-loved diversion of rural society. The live bird was hung up by its feet. Its head and neck were thoroughly greased. The sport consisted of pulling off the bird's head whilst riding at speed. The slaughter of animals was the principal pastime of the nation but not the only one. Horse-racing and cricket grew steadily in popularity; the excitement, natural to both sports, was intensified by furious betting for high stakes. Gambling, indeed, obsessed men and women, rich or poor. Raindrops running down a window pane, the fertility of a dean's wife, steeplechasing by moonlight, anything and everything were grounds for a bet. Amongst the rich stakes ran high—Fox lost two fortunes before middle age; Georgiana Duchess of Devonshire ruined her marriage and herself through her incapacity to restrain her feckless itch to gamble. Craftsmen and shopkeepers were often no more thrifty and reduced their families to penury through a passion for cock-fighting or cricket. The violence, the rioting, the gambling and cruelty were all facets of the Englishman's turbulent nature.

Such strong passions could only flourish amidst a callous people, and it is not surprising that the popular sights of London were the lunatics in Bedlam, the whipping of half-naked women at the Bridewell, the stoning to death of pilloried men and women, or the hangings at Tyburn, where a girl and a boy might be seen dangling between a highwayman and a murderer.[2] A callous attitude to life

[2] Mother Newnham, an aged brothel-keeper, died of the blows received in the pillory in 1731: a boy of sixteen was hanged after the

does not necessarily, however, imply an absence of feeling. Men and women could be easily moved, partly because they lived in a world of passion, tragedy and horror. The rough potters of Burslem and the stunted miners of Cannock Chase were reduced to tears of pity for the lot of man by the intensity of Wesley's compassion. Even the urbane and cynical Chesterfield could not restrain himself from weeping when Whitefield preached. Yet they all accepted the cruelty and violence as a part of the unchanging pattern of life. The reasons are not far to seek—the most powerful, perhaps, was the cheapness of life itself, or rather the lottery of death.

In the midst of the elegance and luxury, dirt and disease abounded. In the reign of George I, and for the early part of that of George II, London was a stinking, muddy, filth-bespattered metropolis, pullulating with slums—St. Giles, Drury Lane, Shoreditch, Alsatia, were full of crowded tenements, the cellars as stuffed with human beings as the attics. Fever of all varieties flourished and infants died like flies; tuberculosis was rampant and took its heavy toll, particularly amongst young mothers. In the 'twenties and 'thirties an abundance of cheap gin proved a dangerous anodyne for the miseries of the poor and deaths increased so alarmingly that even the government was forced to take action and attempt to check its sale. Although death reaped its richest harvest amongst the poor, both in town and country, yet the rich were not immune from its visitations either in their country houses or salubrious suburbs. Smallpox proved a scourge for all classes; appendicitis often killed; fever and consumption, although

---

Gordon riots; Margaret Troke, a girl of sixteen, was burnt at the stake at Winchester in 1738 for poisoning her mistress; John Matthews, a young printer, was hanged, drawn and quartered in 1719 for a very minor treasonable activity.

less frequent amongst the rich, were frequent enough to make life seem a gamble. The prevalence of death and disease sharpened the appetite for life, and more keenly, perhaps, because for many men and women the sense of a future life lost some of its reality.

Men of the time were conscious of both the dirt and the disease and they struggled to overcome them. Smallpox was mastered by inoculation; lying-in hospitals and orphanages made a modest inroad on the appalling wastage of infant mortality. The streets of the great towns grew cleaner and better paved with each passing decade until London had few rivals for cleanliness in Western Europe. An improved water supply, reduction in overcrowding, better personal hygiene, these all helped to reduce the incidence of disease; so did plentiful food which may also have increased human fertility. For these reasons and for others, more strictly economic, there was a very rapid rise in population from the accession of George III that showed some signs of abating by the death of George IV. That in itself helped to complicate the problems of government.

The state machinery was archaic and inefficient, and a part of the brutality and ferocity of life was due to this fact as well as to the prevalence of dirt, disease, and poverty. The government had to preserve order, but the instruments which it possessed were those devised for a more primitive and more scattered society. Parish constables were not much use against a riot in full fury; nor numerous enough to secure a speedy arrest of highwaymen, footpads, pickpockets, and petty thieves who swarmed in the towns and countryside. To counterbalance the lack of certainty in detection, the punishment became heavier. Until the reform of the penal code by Sir Robert Peel, the death penalty was increasingly imposed for crimes against property, yet with no effect. Juries would undervalue

articles to save a felon's life. George III, who took his pre-
rogative of mercy exceedingly seriously, pardoned many
who were afterwards transported to the plantations before
the American colonies were lost, and afterwards to Austra-
lia. Few empires have been founded without the aid of
labour camps and convict settlements. Neither transportation nor hanging deterred the criminal; the chance of
escape bred optimism, a callous attitude to life induced an
indifference to death. Some pleaded for the reform of law
and punishment, putting their faith like Bentham in certainty of capture and solitary confinement; others pleaded
for a sterner retribution—breaking on the wheel, starving
to death, mutilation of the body. So long as the first four
Georges ruled, crime and disorder were the major pre-
occupations of local government. Difficulties were greatly
increased by the attitude of many whose aggressive instincts found satisfaction in the hero-worship of highwaymen and criminals, who expressed by the violence of their
lives a hatred of society, of government, of restraint, which
drew an echoing response from many hearts.

Violence, crime, cruelty, dirt, disease, these were an
indelible part of the Georgian scene. Although their
effects strike us with horror, and occasionally moved even
a contemporary to pity or despair, they were accepted by
the majority of mankind as a part of the nature of life, like
the weather or the seasons. Yet their prevalence made for
a coarser attitude to life and for grosser manners than
many are willing to admit. The language of the court of
George I and II was neither inhibited nor refined; George
IV indulged with his friends in brutal horse-play; the
habits and actions of his brothers were notorious even in
the far from squeamish Regency society. Manners varied
from extreme formality to a freedom which would have
shocked later generations. Augustus Keppel, unable to get

the attention of an attractive girl at a fashionable ball, finally got near enough to her to tug hard at her petti-coats. Even as late as the eighteen-thirties members of Parliament dining at their club fought like schoolboys for their rice pudding, and means had to be found to put a stop to it. Queen Caroline, whose language could be as coarse as any man's, was so shocked by the language which Sir Robert Walpole used to her daughters that she felt constrained to reprimand him. Swift's famous poem on Celia may have been only a mildly funny joke to his con-temporaries. Let anyone who doubts the gross coarseness of the age turn over the cartoons, satires and squibs which poured from the press in such abundance—an exceedingly frank acknowledgement, one might also say a relish, of man's animal functions was as much a part of the age as the elegant furniture or delicate china.

2

The institutions by which this turbulent society was governed were inadequate for their purpose. The machin-ery of law and national government, together with the professions—the Church, the Army, the Navy, and the Law—was largely in the hands of the aristocracy and gentry. Many were hardworking, most had the welfare of their neighbourhood very much at heart, yet few rose above the spirit of the age, which permitted the pursuit of per-sonal interest in the service of the state. The placing of sons, nephews, and cousins in lucrative situations about the court became one of the more serious concerns of politics; such concentration on self-interest bred in the industrious middle classes both a cynical attitude to the institutions of government and a desire to reform them. They hated waste as much as they hated violence and disorder. The manufacturers and tradesmen were in closer touch with their workmen than in later centuries. Men like Josiah Wedgwood, John Wilkinson, and Abraham Darby knew their workmen and their families intimately and were deeply conscious of the tribulations of poverty. They developed a strong patriarchal attitude towards their work-people, whom they wished to discipline like children, for their own sakes. They wanted order, decency, thrift, which they knew well enough were the concomitants of success and prosperity. And they looked for reform from both above and below. They belonged to all movements which encouraged it. They became ardent members of the Society for Reformation of the Manners of the Lower Orders; they worked for the repression of wakes, fairs, and church ales; they suppressed brothels, ale-houses, cock-fighting, and bull-baiting; they founded schools; encouraged libraries; endowed musical festivals; hospitals and orphanages bore their names. They harboured no prejudice against Wesley; they knew too well the efficiency of his work. They were the friends of all men, quakers, dissenters, republicans, reformers—all who believed, as they believed, in endeavour, in the capacity of man to triumph over the disasters and difficulties which beset him, and so create a better world. They resented disorder, incompetence and wasteful expense. They pushed for turnpikes, canals and railways; organised their labour on new lines; kept an open mind and ready purse for inventions. They provided the mind and sinews of England's economy; they, more than any body of men, created the riches which allowed a greater luxury than England had ever known. They knew it, and they wanted England to be governed in accordance with those principles whose value had been clearly demonstrated, they felt, by their own success. Although the majority of them had a profound sense of the law of subordination and were not unmindful of the traditions of their country, they did not reverence the past for its own sake. They were entranced by the prospect of the future. They desired to build a better world and became impatient of hindrance. These leaders of industry, great or small, are to be found in the late eighteenth and early nineteenth centuries in every movement for reform. They read Bentham, Priestley, Romilly, Wilberforce, Howard, Cartwright; read and believed what they read, and confidently placed their money and their time at the disposal of those who wished to create a more ordered, hard-working, decent and just society; a society based on industry, thrift, and godliness.

There are few more typical figures than Samuel Whitbread. From modest origins he created a fortune by the rationalisation and development of his brewery. His success led not to a conservative attitude to life but to a passionate support of any movement for reform, one of the most necessary of which he considered to be the increase of political liberty for the masses. Believing passionately in the capacity of his own age to outmatch the artistic triumphs of former times, he commissioned Henry Holland to remodel his old house at Southill, Bedfordshire, and to design the furnishing, the decoration, and the gardens to harmonise with the house. The result is one of the most complete works of art of the Georgian age. The opulence and beauty of the house must be seen in relation to the library in order to assess properly the full measure of the man.

> . . . the political career of the builder of Southill is best illustrated in the remarkable series of pamphlets of the late eighteenth and early nineteenth centuries. Pre-eminent in certain subjects such as the Slave

Trade, Poor Law Reform and the education of the
working classes, the collection covers `all the vital
questions of that momentous quarter of a century—
the French Revolution, the Napoleonic and American
Wars, Catholic Emancipation and the Regency, and it
includes many first editions . . . of such authors as
Jeremy Bentham, Edmund Burke, Thomas Clarkson,
T. R. Malthus, Tom Paine, Joseph Priestley and
Arthur Young.[8]

Behind Whitbread and Wedgwood and other great
figures of industrial and commercial life were humbler
men, small manufacturers, artisans, shopkeepers, and
craftsmen who met together and discussed as earnestly as
their betters the need to reform the world and the turbulent life of their time. Thrift, sobriety, self-help;
eupeptic optimism; an unshakeable belief in the rational,
these are as much a part of Georgian life as the disease, the
dirt, the violence, and the cruelty. The early years of
George I's reign are notable for a remarkable development
in primary education and in the widespread growth of
societies to reform manners: the closing years of George
IV's reign, with its proliferating mechanics' institutes and
literary and scientific societies, indicate that men had not
lost their faith in the powers of education and possibly of
reformation.

3

There was one further strand in Georgian society that re-
quires notice; in many ways the strongest and the most
durable. The bulk of the population avoided the excess
and the ebullience, looked neither forwards nor back-

[8] *Southill, A Regency House*, The Library, by A. N. L. Munby, 64.

wards, but lived instinctively according to the ancient ways
of their fathers, content with those institutions which had
ruled them for generations. They were only involved, as
the majority of mankind will always be, in the ever-
renewing drama of personal existence. They accepted
poverty or riches, disease or health, work or idleness as
they came. Each perhaps cherished his ambition, his ideals,
his frustrations and anxieties, but kept them in a tight
personal framework as he did his happiness and joy. Gray
wrote of these men in lines which have now become platitudinous but once were alive and fresh,

> Far from the madding crowd's ignoble strife
> Their sober wishes never learn'd to stray;
> Along the cool sequester'd vale of life
> They kept the noiseless tenor of their way.

Free and mobile as the English society was, compared with
other European countries, it was nevertheless very rigid
by modern standards. The theme of many people's lives
was fixed by birth. They stayed in the village in which
they were born and pursued those avocations in which their
fathers and grandfathers had been employed. These un-
awakened masses were the despair of the reformers; yet to
the rulers of the country they were the ballast of society,
the salt of England. They filled the hamlets, villages,
market towns; some of the great cities contained many
craftsmen's families who were untouched by ideas either
political or economic: they were content to live and to
work according to their ancient rule. The wide distribu-
tion of such men and women, to whom the names of
Wesley, Walpole, and North, let alone Bentham, Wilberforce, or Paine, may easily have been unknown, goes far to
explain why such a restless society, in which new forces
were working like yeast, should have maintained its archaic
institutions of government for so long. It is easier to

understand, too, when it is remembered that food was quite plentiful and reasonably cheap for most years between 1714 to 1790, not perhaps by present standards but by the standards of the time. Poverty and hunger were not uncommon but few starved to death.

This attitude of acceptance was naturally encouraged by those who found the Georgian world much to their advantage. There were many who did, and oddly enough they grew more numerous as George followed George; thus the forces of conservatism strengthened during the same period as the forces of reform. During the rule of the first Hanoverians there was much grumbling, even in those institutions naturally attached to the state—the Church and the Universities. The clergy, bred in the traditions of non-resistance and the divine right of kings, looked askance at their German monarchs and hankered in a half-hearted way for the Stuarts. Few were actively disloyal but the majority enjoyed the diatribes of the opposition press, relishing its denunciation of corruption in high places. The bulk of the gentry felt the same. They had no hope of cutting a figure at Court themselves and they affected to despise their aristocratic neighbours who did, unless they happened to be related to them and could expect a few pickings for themselves. Time, prosperity, and the threats to the traditional pattern of society which arise in the middle decades of the eighteenth century modified their attitude and changed them into ardent supporters of the *status quo*, as absolute for church and state as Dr. Johnson himself. George III, unlike his great-grandfather, had few subjects more loyal than his clergy or gentry. After all life was good for them. Few clergy lived in want; here and there a squire drifted into bankruptcy; but the majority enjoyed, like Parson Woodforde or Squire Allworthy, an income appropriate to their station, and the authority due to their wealth. It is not surprising that they discovered spiritual virtues of the highest order in the hierarchic nature of society. They read Soame Jenyn's *Free Enquiry into the Nature and Origin of Evil* with approval, agreeing that " the beauty and happiness of the whole depend on the just inferiority of the parts ". He pointed out to them that just as the lower animals enjoyed their ignorant bliss, so the human poor were happy in their inferior way. " Ignorance is the opiate of the poor, a cordial administered by the kindly purposes of Providence." Education and change were ill-judged, irrational, inimical to the wise designs of Providence. Jenyns merely states more blatantly the implications embedded in Burke's beautiful and ornate prose. The slow growth of society was the work of time and history, imperfections as well as perfections were but a part of the mysterious Providential process. Reason dictated acceptance; reason shunned rapid change; reforms except the gentlest were to be avoided. Blackstone proved with monumental erudition that the chaotic and archaic system of English law expressed the most perfect legal wisdom. Paley demonstrated that the *status quo* was in accordance with the precepts of Christian theology. That *reason* upon which the reformer relied was used with equal dexterity by those who found the world comfortable to their purpose.

The doctrines of Burke, Blackstone, Jenyns, Paley, and lesser writers found a ready response in the thousand and one little oligarchies which stretched like a fine network across the length and breadth of the land. Within all merchant communities, economic, social, and political power tended to drift into the hands of a few closely interrelated families. The great merchant princes of the city of London were almost as closely intermarried as the aristocracy, and their economic and financial interests were curiously uniform. The same names occur in the directorates of the Bank, the East India, and South Sea Companies; they are to be found in insurance, banking and every form of overseas trade. Bristol, Norwich, Hull, Newcastle, Liverpool present the same picture in miniature. The wealth of these groups was of commercial rather than industrial origin; the accumulation of their riches had not been hindered by the structure of government or the lack of social discipline, so that by and large they were content—at least until the end of the eighteenth century—with the world as they found it. There were a few dissidents amongst them, as there were too amongst the aristocracy, but the age was too individualistic, too aggressive for a smooth uniformity. Yet it is wrong to think of all of this class of merchants and *entrepreneurs* as radically minded. Those who came from families of established wealth and who had won control of their corporations or their cities had little cause for discontent. And such was true of the attorneys, doctors, general merchants and prosperous farmers of the little market boroughs. Jealousy and antipathy might be rife amongst themselves, particularly in those excluded from power, but the successful quickly learnt to exploit the comfortable sinecures and the extensive charities which a kindly Providence had placed in their keeping. To these men change was an anathema—ancient ways were sanctified. Poverty, dirt, disease, crime were a part of the nature of the universe—mysterious yet inevitable, and certainly beyond man's competence. The most that man could hope to do to assuage these evils was to exercise charity and benevolence. Whatever the cause—self-interest, ignorance, or indifference—the bulk of the population was prepared to accept life as they found it. This core of acceptance created a valuable ballast in the state at a time when the forces of order were of so flimsy a nature, and when the proselytisers of reform were frequently rash, violent, and unrestrained.

Yet so archaic were many institutions of government that a more violent clash with the party of reform could scarcely have been avoided, in spite of the lethargy of most of the nation, had not there been times of prolonged prosperity. The disaster of the American War of Independence strengthened immensely the reformers' hands and brought the government system into jeopardy; yet those disasters, considered economically, were more apparent than real. Had England suffered the repeated defeats of France, then reform might easily have turned into revolution. As it was, growing prosperity dulled the edge of criticism. The growth of wealth was never smooth nor continuous; its incidence was apt to be irregular, constant wars produced violent reactions in the uncontrolled economic system, and men of great wisdom and foresight at times prognosticated national ruin. The ruin never came, instead the visible signs of wealth multiplied exceedingly; few nations have grown so rapidly in prosperity as the Britain of the first four Georges. This was due to the development of commerce and industry, which, in turn, were greatly stimulated by the aggressive wars in which the country was so frequently involved.

4

In 1714 England was a country of small towns and scattered population; the wealth of its people did not compare with that of the French or Dutch. Europe had been amazed by the resilience of English economy during the long wars of the Spanish Succession, which indicated unexpected reserves of wealth. Throughout the seventeenth century there had taken place a steady development of her resources. Agrarian techniques had improved greatly; corn, wool, hides had increased in production; the exploitation of coal stimulated industry at home and exports abroad. The growth of ship-building created a merchant navy which was trying to rival the Dutch and to wrest from them a considerable portion of the world's carrying trade. The plantations of America provided admirably protected markets for infant British industries and produced raw materials of exceptional value—sugar, tobacco, furs, fish, and timber. At the same time they created a market for slaves and also absorbed some of the more undesirable elements of English society—criminals, whores, and bankrupts.

This agrarian and commercial revolution stimulated England's prosperity and created a profound belief in the benefits to be derived from overseas trade. The great stumbling-block to England's hopes was France, and more particularly France in alliance with Spain, for Spain's possessions in the New World twinkled like *El Dorado* in the eyes of British merchants. Early in Charles II's reign many Englishmen had come to realise that France was England's great rival. They welcomed William III and rejoiced in the War of the Spanish Succession, and their bitterness knew no bounds when they witnessed the failure of Harley and Bolingbroke to seize the fruits of Marlborough's great victories. The total humiliation of France and the commercial supremacy of the world seemed within the nation's grasp in 1710. From 1713 to 1739 there was peace; peace which to many was degrading, a peace which made Britain the dupe of France which, under the cloak of friendship, was steadily rebuilding its maritime and industrial strength for the inevitable clash. Large sections of mercantile opinion howled for war and repeated with delight the elder Pitt's fulminations against the supine policy of Walpole which sacrificed the glorious prospect of empire for the sake of the King's beggarly Electorate. Hanover, they thought, was the millstone round poor England's neck, dragging it down to a cowardly ignominy. War came. And for the rest of their time on the throne the Georges enjoyed but few years of peace. And the country thrived on war. Although one empire was lost, another far greater was won. The mining of coal, the forging of iron and steel, the weaving of cloth, the building of ships, the making of sail, were nourished by war. Trade flourished; innovations and improvements which might lead to an increase in production were eagerly sought. Wasteful methods, lack of discipline amongst workers, idleness, drunkenness, and social disorder were frowned upon. Rivers were made navigable, canals cut, roads improved; the successful development of the steam engine led to further revolutions in the application of power. By the time George IV died the railway age had begun and industrial England had been successfully born. War had been its midwife.

5

The effects of the industrial revolution on social life have been misunderstood. It was achieved only by a great increase in population and by more efficient organisation of society. The reasons for the increase of population are complex; greater economic opportunity may have led to earlier marriages and earlier breeding; better food to an increase of fertility. There was also a conscious effort made to improve social hygiene and to keep alive the young. More of the labouring classes lived for longer and that fact also increased the sum of human happiness. Furthermore, bad as many of the conditions of life were for the labouring classes, they were often better than the poor had enjoyed in Western Europe since Roman times. Hunger was common, starvation not unknown, bad harvests could and did create terrible conditions. Nevertheless, by 1830 the mass of the population was eating more varied foods than had been enjoyed by its great-great-grandfathers. They lived too in better houses, and if they worked more systematically and got drunk less frequently they made up in security what they lost in liberty. The comparative prosperity of the labouring classes and their ever-increasing numbers were a further stimulus to that revolution in industry and trade of which they were the sinews. They created a great home market for food, for clothing, and for the simple luxuries of life.

Only a sprinkling of the new wealth dribbled through to the poor; the bulk was absorbed by the aristocracy, the gentry, and the growing middle class. Indeed one of the greatest changes brought about by the industrial revolution took place in the way the middle class lived. Merchants, shopkeepers, small industrialists, the factors and attorneys lived on intimate terms with their craftsmen and clerks who, at times, shared their houses. They were often educated at the same schools, first the dame's school, then the local grammar school. Their wives and daughters possessed some finery and usually a maid, but much of their lives was spent in the same domestic pursuits as that of the wives of their workpeople. Merchants' wives, as they prospered, had always been prone to ape gentility—the social comedies of the seventeenth and eighteenth centuries are full of such women—but these were regarded as comic, as foolish, as reaching far beyond their stations. By the last half of the eighteenth century, however, the pursuit of refinement and gentility was endowed with moral virtue. The contrasts between Mrs. Bennett and her daughters illustrates the gulf between the generations.

The middle classes could afford refinement. They had the money to go to Bath, to Tunbridge Wells, to Harrogate, to spend money on clothes, on china, on furniture, on silver and plate. They created an active market for the enterprising craftsman. Fortunately they were willing to spend their wealth on objects where mass production was difficult or in its infancy, and the reigns of George III and IV were a golden age for the English craftsman. The middle classes grew exceedingly prosperous and the countryside was dotted with elegant villas, filled with pleasing copies of Chippendale or Sheraton; Wedgwood, Spode, Worcester, or Derby china filled the cabinets and the side-boards; excellent silver and the new Sheffield plate gave an air of gentility to the table. The food was massive, the wines abundant, labour cheap; yet it was easy to live within one's income, easy to save, easy to plan for the prosperous generations to come. It is not surprising that the world of Jane Austen should have fascinated generations of middle-class readers, or that this late-Georgian period should have been dubbed the "Age of Elegance".

If it was the "Age of Elegance" for the middle class, it was the "Age of Grandeur" for the nobility and gentry. Towards the end of the eighteenth century their incomes began to rise sharply—not that most of them had been poor or hard-pressed in its earlier decades. It was partly due to the increased prosperity of agriculture—the rentals of the Earl of Egremont's estates in Yorkshire rose from £12,976 in 1791 to £34,000 in 1824 and those in Sussex from £7,950 to £14,770.[4] They were made richer by the

[4] A. A. Wyndham, *A Family History*, II, 300-1.

industrial revolution, for many discovered valuable minerals on their estates. They were quick to put their money in the funds, to speculate in real property, in shipping and in industry—after it had proved its worth, although a few such as the Duke of Bridgewater were pioneers of economic enterprise. Rich as their grandfathers had been they were richer. The prosperity of the nobility was such that they could buy whatever the world had to offer; the gentry could not be so lavish, but even they could afford fine pictures and were rich enough to rebuild their houses and landscape their gardens according to aristocratic fashion.

Yet they were *nouveaux riches* and had little or no faith in the artistic achievements of their own country or in its efflorescence of science, of thought, and to a lesser extent of art. The late seventeenth century knew Newton, Locke, and Wren, three men of genius; few countries in Europe could boast their equals. Painters were lacking but Grinling Gibbons had brought the art of decoration to a point where it could stand comparison with the best in Europe. Yet somehow there was no development, no increase in stature, no burgeoning of a culture, literary, scientific, or artistic, which could compare with France; at times even the Dutch and Italians seemed far superior. Certainly the aristocracy had little confidence in their country's culture. They bought the majority of their pictures in Italy and France, leaving only their portraits to be painted by English painters. Their furniture was French or modelled by English craftsmen in French or Italian styles. Their houses were designed according to the principles of Palladio or other Italians masters; their decoration was largely the work of foreign artists—Artari, Verrio, Laguerre, Kauffmann, Rysbrack. And the ancient world held them almost equally in thrall—the civilisations of Greece and Rome epitomised the virtues which they sought. A sound classical education became essential for a gentleman, and to acquire fashionable manners and elegant taste the gay aristocrat was despatched on a Grand Tour of France and Italy. Few returned without a desire to embellish their homes, and the result is the magnificent heritage of Britain's Georgian houses. Although the inspiration for these was frequently foreign, subtle modifications made them curiously apt in their English settings. Also the passion for collecting old masters and antique sculpture helped undeniably to establish a British school of painting, not only of singular excellence in portraiture, but in Constable and Turner discovering painters of landscape who could compare almost favourably with the best in France or Italy. Yet it should never be forgotten that the eighteenth-century Englishman was rich rather than cultured, possessing little faith in the artistic achievements of his own country and cherishing an excessive respect both for the art of France and Italy and for the glories of Greece and Rome.

6

The first four Georges ruled for a little over one hundred years, yet they witnessed far profounder changes in economic, social, and cultural life than any previous monarchs. During these times England ceased to be a small influential maritime state and became the leading empire of the world, responsible for the destinies of scores of millions of mankind. In 1830 no country in the world could match her wealth nor challenge her industrial supremacy. Such a triumph was bound to create arrogance. It was difficult for Englishmen not to feel that Providence itself had ordained that they should rule and impose their will on less fortunate races of men. In the eighteenth century their wealth had created envy; in the early nineteenth their moral pride made them hated. Hostility creates isolation; and Englishmen took refuge in their obvious worldly success. The maintenance of English ways, the insistence on the superiority of English ideas, led to a withdrawal from European culture as a whole and England in the nineteenth century developed its art and its literature almost uninfluenced by foreign example. The attitude of inferiority of the eighteenth century was transformed into the complacent arrogance of the nineteenth and England, not Europe, was the loser. The confidence to which such a sense of superiority gave rise has led also to a distortion of the magnitude of English achievement in the Georgian age. It was formidable in technology, but in science and mathematics it could scarcely compare with European achievement, and in all the arts, save perhaps for the poetry of the romantic revival, it was very definitely inferior. Here and there—Gibbon and perhaps Hume—there is a writer of European stature, but the general level of achievement in philosophy, history, and literature is mediocre. Painting and music tell the same story. The decorative arts are equally jejune and provincial: Vincennes and Sèvres have no rivals amongst English ceramics, just as Chippendale and Sheraton cannot compare with the *ébénistes* who worked for Louis XV. Half the attraction of Georgian art is due to the absolute poverty of what came before and of what came after—an oasis of beauty between the monstrosities of the Jacobean and the horrors of the Victorian. Rich enough to afford to imitate the best, eighteenth-century England lacked the confidence to create its own standards of taste and culture. Behind the braggart attitude there was an inner uncertainty, a sense of being provincial which ever-growing prosperity could not disguise. In many ways England in the eighteenth century in its attitude to things European was similar to that of Rome in the first century to Greece or America in the late nineteenth to Europe—too conscious both of its own riches and its own rawness.

CHAPTER II

GEORGE I

1714—1727

The accession of George I took place in an atmosphere of intense drama. From the spring of 1714 Queen Anne had been ailing, her huge moribund bulk was gradually crushing the feeble life within. Her ministry was Tory. Her Lord Treasurer, the Earl of Oxford and Mortimer, better known as Robert Harley, was a guileful, moderate man, willing to play almost any game which kept him in power and dished his hated rival Henry St. John, Viscount Bolingbroke, the Secretary of State. These two colleagues had grown to loathe each other. The prevarications and intrigues of Harley with moderate Whigs and moderate Tories had driven Bolingbroke to seek his allies amongst the violent and intemperate country gentlemen who were quite willing to entertain the idea of bringing back the Stuarts, particularly so if James III could be persuaded to give up allegiance to Rome—an act which Bolingbroke thought he could accomplish. This brilliant, unstable man had little conception of the rugged and obstinate adherence to religion which characterised the later Stuarts, otherwise he might have curbed his extravagance. And yet to have done so would have meant compromise with the detestable Harley and perhaps with the even more detestable Whigs who had no use for him at all.

The Tories had never been strong enough to govern without the help of some politicians who were whiggishly inclined. The most important of these was the Duke of

Shrewsbury, a man of poor health and great acumen, to whom William III had frequently turned in his difficulties. Shrewsbury hated office and avoided it, but at times his conscience forced him to accept. In 1710 the intransigence of Marlborough and those Whigs who had wished to prolong the war against France had forced him back into office in order to support Harley in his quest for peace. The quarrels of Oxford and Bolingbroke, and fears that the latter might easily betray the Revolution of 1688 by an act of supreme folly, had kept him in office. Shrewsbury belonged to an ancient aristocratic family; Oxford was the son of a country squire, so was Bolingbroke. Queen Anne felt far closer to Shrewsbury, her Lord Chamberlain, than she did to her two chief ministers.

Sick as she was, she was forced by habit and custom to preside at the weekly meetings of her cabinet which were held at court every Sunday after dinner. Bolingbroke and Harley grew increasingly quarrelsome and at last their hatred for each other flared into an open brawl in the Queen's presence. To make matters worse, Oxford was obviously quite drunk. Nagged by her confidants and driven beyond endurance she took away Oxford's white staff—his badge of office as Lord Treasurer. This took place on 27 July 1714. The news put London in a ferment. Would Bolingbroke succeed Oxford? Did this mean a Jacobite succession?

No sooner had London been filled with speculation than it was learnt that the Queen was dying. Would Bolingbroke have time to secure his party in power even if he obtained the White Staff? Then it was learnt that Bolingbroke was dining with Sunderland, Stanhope, and the leading Whigs. The Privy Council met, and possibly with the connivance of Shrewsbury, the Dukes of Argyll and Somerset, both Whigs and loyal Hanoverians, attended. Bolingbroke was cornered; the dying Queen made Shrewsbury Lord Treasurer and the crisis was over. Time, if nothing else, had defeated the Jacobites and made George I's accession certain. Young Craggs was despatched, even before the Queen was dead, to ask George to hasten to England. As he rode to Hanover, Oxford, ever hopeful, wrote a long letter to Bothmer, the new King's confidential adviser, expressing a hope that the King would rule without party. Neither George nor his ministers had any such intention; the Whigs had been loyal to the House of Hanover and they were to reap their reward. Such loyal Tories as the Earl of Nottingham were found minor offices. Marlborough was reinstated as Captain-General of the Forces. But the great offices of state were given to those Whig nobles who were called the Junto.

2

King George did not hurry. Like most of his race he possessed an almost pathological concern for detail and he knew himself to be leaving Hanover for a long time. By the middle of September his stately retinue got under way, only to be stopped time and time again to receive the congratulations of mayors and burghers of the cities through which he passed. In Holland there were receptions and addresses, and it was not until 27 September that the royal yacht, flanked by Dutch and English men-of-war, set out for the Thames. It arrived on 29 September in thick fog which was so bad the next morning that the King had to be rowed up the river to Greenwich in his barge, arriving there only after nightfall. Everyone who could afford it had hurriedly left London to get a sight of their new King.

The beautiful buildings of Wren made a perfect setting for the King's reception, and the candles and the torchlight picked out in a blaze of colour the fine satin and velvet, as the nobility of England waited to do homage. Even Ormonde was there—for long in correspondence with James over the water—and Oxford, too, lurked on the fringe of the crowd hoping to be noticed. No one paid much attention to them. The King was particularly gracious to Marlborough, saying to him in French, " My dear Duke, I hope you have now seen the end of your troubles." The old Archbishop of Canterbury, an ardent Whig and for some years ignored both by Queen and Ministry, tried out his rusty French in a speech of welcome. Those who had made their court at Hanover were the centres of exciting, gossiping crowds, eager to learn what their new master was like.

George I was fifty-four years of age when he ascended the English throne. Short, fair-skinned, he possessed the bright blue bulbous eyes and irascible expression of the Guelphs—two traits of the family face which were to descend generation after generation. Bred a soldier, he carried into Court some of the peremptory habits of the field. He was brave, obstinate, and shy. Very stupid and lacking interest in the arts, save music, he was nevertheless far from being a nonentity. His character was strong and powerful and complex, and although he was lazy he had no intention of being ruled by his ministers. He was not in any way enamoured of his new subjects. They had an evil reputation amongst monarchs for shiftiness. His own family had been insulted by Anne and her ministers. He was aware that most of the noblemen who fawned upon him at his arrival had dabbled in treason. He put his trust in Bothmer and Bernstorff, two life-long Hanoverian servants, and the quick-witted Huguenot refugee, Robethon, who had been William III's private secretary. The English courtiers were quick to realise their importance; for a time they did not resent it, and courted them obsequiously.

There was no Queen : she had been divorced. Bored by her husband and irked by his infidelities, Sophia Dorothy of Celle had listened too eagerly to the supplications of a handsome adventurer—Königsmarck. She was prepared to elope with him. Then Königsmarck vanished. His body was never found, and almost certainly he was murdered. At the time of his disappearance George was in Berlin and cannot have been directly responsible for his death. On 28 December 1694 Sophia Dorothy was divorced and shut up in the Castle of Ahlden where she remained until her death thirty-two years later. Never again did she set eyes on her husband or children. George ignored her appeals for pardon. Such a story provided the courts of Europe with decades of gossip and speculation. It added a touch of the sinister to George's character and certainly enhanced his attraction in the eyes of many women of his Court.

George had a healthy animal appetite for women. He preferred them fat and complacent. As he was a man of habit he grew attached to one or two of them, and amongst these Ehrengard Melusina von Schulenburg, afterwards Duchess of Kendal, came to be regarded as *maîtresse en titre*. By the time she arrived in England she was nearly sixty, a tall, thin, bony woman who had grown more interested in money and power than in the delights of the flesh. The King, however, was used to her and spent long hours in her apartments, which were on the ground floor of St. James's Palace, facing the garden; there he indulged, amongst other pleasures, his passion for cutting out paper figures. When not with the Duchess of Kendal, the King was usually to be found with Charlotte Sophia Kielmannsegge, afterwards Countess of Darlington.[1] Physically she provided a delightful contrast to the Duchess. No one has bettered Horace Walpole's description of her. When he was a young boy she made a violent impression on him.

Lady Darlington, whom I saw at my mother's in my infancy, and whom I remember by being terrified at her enormous figure, was as corpulent and ample as the Duchess was long and emaciated. Two fierce black eyes, large and rolling beneath two lofty arched eyebrows, two acres of cheeks spread with crimson, an ocean of neck that overflowed and was not distinguished from the lower parts of her body, and no part restrained by stays—no wonder that a child dreaded such an ogress, and that the mob of London were highly diverted at the importation of so uncommon a seraglio!

Yet the Kielmannsegge was not without a certain charm. She was vivacious, moderately well read, friendly, eager to please. There can be no doubt that these two mistresses did much to enliven the Court, although the public did not take to them very kindly. The man in the street assumed at once that the King was in their toils and that they exploited him for their own sinister purposes. As Mist wrote in his *Journal* on 27 May 1721. "We are ruined by trulls, nay, what is more vexatious, by old ugly trulls, such as could not find entertainment in the most hospitable hundreds of old Drury."

[1] She was the daughter of the Countess of Platen, mistress to George I's father. Some historians, notably Sir Adolphus Ward, have exonerated her from the charge of being George I's mistress on the grounds that she may have been his illegitimate half-sister—hence her influence at his Court. Owing to the extreme promiscuity of her mother, her paternity must have been too speculative to have restrained George I, for no contemporary, not even his daughter-in-law, doubted that she was his mistress. Her production of a certificate of fidelity, signed by her husband, failed to dispel their suspicions.

There was some truth in the jibe. Both mistresses were rapacious, both probably took bribes. George I was an indolent man, and allowed them to exploit their position. They were kept a little in check by a lack of certainty in the King's affections. He was quickly influenced and he had not been in England long before his roving eye caught the Duchess of Shrewsbury, a lively, ribald Italian, who enjoyed her success hugely.

George's Court might be rather coarse and earthy, but it was a vast improvement on the dismal last years of Anne's, and courtiers flocked to St. James's as much for the fun as for the power politics—at least for a time. Once the King had settled in, however, he became increasingly elusive to all but his Hanoverian advisers and English ministers, save for a few intimate friends. He was a shy man and an obstinate one, and he liked living his life on his own terms, which did not include levées and drawing-room circles. He preferred living in two rooms, and being looked after by his servants, Mohammed and Mustapha, whom he had captured, as a young man, in his campaign against the Turks. When he went to the opera, of which he was very fond, he preferred to avoid the Royal Box. His other amusement was gambling, but again he did not like to sit down at cards with his Court. He went off *incognito* to the house of a friend and played, unwatched, with a few of his cronies.

His personality and age were such that these habits could not be changed, and the Court, much brighter though it might be than Anne's, would quickly have ceased to be the centre of social life but for the Prince and Princess of Wales. They loved company and the Princess, Caroline of Ansbach, was one of the liveliest of women, one, indeed, who would have been outstanding in any walk of life. Her husband, afterwards George II, was much like his father, much more like him than he would have cared to admit, for they both loathed each other. No doubt the Prince of Wales bore some resentment against his father for his treatment of his mother, if not of her lover. And for Princes Kings tend to live too long and enjoy their power too thoroughly. George I conducted a campaign of well-directed snubs against his son. On the eve of their journey to England he had ordered his grandson, Frederick, to be left behind, and Caroline travelled after them with her three daughters. Actions such as these were always reducing the Prince to paroxysms of rage: there was nothing that he could do about it—after all he had been reared to regard Kings as quite specially important. Fuming and impatient he awaited the day when the throne would be his. His actions and words betrayed too frequently his hope that this would not be far distant—an attitude which did nothing to dispel the vexation which the sight of him aroused in the King.

The King's relations with the Princess were better. She possessed ample charms. A bosom of exemplary magnitude was encased in the fairest and pinkest of skins. Her hair was fine, flaxen, abundant; her eyes sky-blue; her features heavy but good. Indeed she was the type of woman the King found hard to resist. In this he was not alone, and the Princess was well aware that she was extremely physically attractive to many men, including her husband, which added immensely both to her poise and to her coquetry. Also she was highly intelligent, fond to indulgence of theological speculation, and her sharpened wits were ever ready to establish a conversational advantage. The King, drawn irresistibly by her charms, not infrequently received a dexterous verbal buffet for his pains. Although he called her " *Cette diablesse Madame la Princesse* " he never bore her any ill-will. But for Caroline the state of affairs in the royal family would have been more intolerable than it was. Harmony, however, was preserved for a time by the excitement and novelty of the accession and by the sudden threat of disaster which came in its wake.

3

In 1714 the Whigs had made the best of their advantage. After four years out of office, during which several of them had been publicly humiliated, they came to power determined to crush Queen Anne's late advisers for good and all. Halifax, Sunderland, Stanhope, Townshend, and Walpole were not men given to half measures. Marlborough, whose nature might have inclined him towards a middle course, was old and not disposed to charity by the treatment which he had received. The rest took the simple view that the Treaty of Utrecht was a national humiliation by which the fruits of Marlborough's victories had been thrown away for the secret purpose of appeasing France and of restoring the Pretender. Almost totally in charge of the administration, they were able to prepare so thoroughly for the general election which by the provisions of an Act of Parliament took place within six months of the Queen's death that they acquired a most handsome majority. That achieved, they set up a Secret Committee of the Commons to investigate the past and bring traitors to book. The Committee's powers were widened to enable them to arrest suspects. Oxford viewed these developments with despondency, Bolingbroke with alarm. On 6 April 1715 he slipped out of the theatre before the end of the play and

went over to St. Germain to join the Pretender. Four
months later Ormonde joined him there; Oxford preferred
the Tower.

The elections, although favourable to the Whigs, had
not been free from Jacobite riots. The Union with Scotland, achieved in 1707, had created much resentment, particularly in the Highlands. Peace had brought its usual
problems—unemployment and disbanded soldiery, made
worse by insufficient harvests. The forceful uprooting of
Tories, great or small, whether in national or local government, turned their thoughts, naturally enough, to rebellion. Few counties lacked a handful of half-bankrupt
gentry willing to risk their necks in a great gamble. Ireland, indestructibly Catholic, was unlikely to remain
quiescent, in spite of the battering which it had received
from William III, if the Pretender obtained a foothold.
James also had a general and a politician of the first rank.
A Stuart invasion became a matter of time. Indolent
he might be, nevertheless George I had to spend many
hours with his cabinet, putting his Kingdom in a posture
of defence.

He was well served by his ministry. The revolt, when it
broke out, was limited to Scotland, yet there were many
dangerous moments, and the "Fifteen" has been too
readily dismissed as a fiasco. The two Hanoverian generals
—Argyll and Cadogan—were at loggerheads; vile weather
hampered the despatch of heavy artillery from the Thames,
which froze. The presence of Dutch soldiers aroused
bitterness wherever they marched. And for five months a
Jacobite army was in control of a most considerable part
of Scotland. A situation was created which was fraught
with danger for the Hanoverian succession. The defeat
of the rebels at Sheriffmuir, and the return of the Chevalier
to France brought infinite relief to the Court. The throne

of George I was safe, at least for a time, but a lurking threat remained, and the shadow of civil war was cast across the early years of his rule.

The accession, followed quickly by the Fifteen, had kept George's ministry hard at work, and to all appearances harmonious. No sooner had James III got back to France than quarrels began between the King's advisers. They started over the question of punishment of those Scots lords who had been captured. Nottingham and others pleaded for clemency; Walpole and Townshend wanted to see their heads on Temple Bar; so did the King. Yet it was important that the King should seem merciful. Some of the more intransigent Whigs pleaded that the King under the Act of Settlement could not pardon impeached traitors—ingenious, but bad law. In the end two were executed (one, Derwentwater, was a grandson of Charles II); one escaped and three were respited, much to the King's irritation. And Nottingham left the cabinet. The brief ministerial harmony was over and for the next six years George I was plagued with one ministerial crisis after another.

It was partly his own fault and partly the predicament in which he found himself. The Tories were broken and disgraced; Oxford was in the Tower, Bolingbroke in France with the Pretender; Nottingham had failed, as he had done for most of his life, to become an influential figure at Court. The field was clear for the great Whig magnates. But which? Already there were several clearly defined groups, each eager to betray the other and secure supreme power for itself. One of the causes of this lack of unity was the death of many of the great Whig figures of the past two reigns; Wharton died in 1715, both Somers and Halifax a year later. Godolphin had been dead for some time, Marlborough had aged very considerably, and was quite moribund. The men who had dominated politics for a generation had passed away, those who were left lacked the strength or the following to control the younger, ambitious men who were quite willing to risk the national security in a struggle for supreme power. The leaders of the three major groups were Sunderland, Townshend, and Argyll. Sunderland had been bred to the Court. His father had been minister to Charles II, James II, and William III, a dexterous, ambitious and pliable man. The young Sunderland had been married into the great families, first Newcastle,[2] then Marlborough. Wealthy, intelligent, a man of strong passions, he was impatient of rivals and expected to receive the King's trust. Yet he was subtle enough to dissimulate and, unlike his father, he had a genius for timing when to strike. His rise to power had been interrupted more frequently than might have been expected, largely because in Anne's reign he had been implacably Whiggish in his opinions and outspoken in their utterance. At that time he was a young man, serving an ageing Queen, and so could afford the luxury of unbending Whiggery. Sunderland had been bred to greatness—and George I was very keen on a man's breeding. Also Sunderland spoke French easily and well. He possessed a wide knowledge of European courts, and the King could chat with him at his ease—quite a rare situation in this new and very insular court. Argyll and Townshend contrasted strongly with Sunderland. Argyll was a soldier, a good and brave one, but eaten alive with jealousy of Marlborough. Indeed he had spent most of the campaign against the Jacobites quarrelling viciously with Cadogan, the other commander, who happened to be a friend and protégé of Marlborough's. His politics had always been of the dodging kind; no sooner did one group think they

[2] Of the first, not the second, creation.

had got him, than he would slip away to another to force up his importance and his price. Few liked him, fewer trusted him, and his pretensions had been largely ignored at the accession. He knew the moves and accordingly he had made himself agreeable to the Prince and obnoxious to the Germans; he could be relied upon to create the maximum trouble given half an opportunity. His power was far from negligible, for he and his brother controlled a great deal of the political world of Scotland. Their family had a long history of treason.

Charles Viscount Townshend was, however, more dangerous a rival to Sunderland than Argyll. A rough, passionate man, he was far harder working than Sunderland and, if less intelligent, more efficient. His outlook was English not European and he had sufficient experience of diplomacy to make his politics sound informed, as well as realistic, to the common run of politicians. He had the advantage of being supported by his formidable brother-in-law, Robert Walpole, who possessed a character of astonishing force and the ability to use it to the full. In the Commons there was no one who could compare with him. He cultivated a blunt, forthright manner in which coarseness of speech was at one with his vast, red, bucolic appearance. After a brief honeymoon with the Germans at the accession, the two brothers-in-law had begun to lose ground at Court. They were an ill-bred pair, neither of them adept at French, and they so obviously wanted to dominate their fellow men that they incurred hostility wherever they went. Although their insularity was a disadvantage at Court, it appealed to the majority of Englishmen, who took a low view of German monarchs, German mistresses, and German advisers. Amongst those members of both Houses of Parliament who could never expect to hold office, they were popular.

Across these groups fell the shadow of James Stanhope
—friend to all, committed to none. Townshend and
Walpole were quite convinced of his loyalty. He had
some of the bluffness and heartiness that they admired, and
they had been friendly for most of their lives. They were
deluded. Everything in his temperament drew Stanhope
to Sunderland's orbit. Grandson of the Earl of Chesterfield, he had grown up in Madrid, where his father was
ambassador. Although he had been bred to the profession
of arms, he was far more cultivated than the majority of
soldiers. Like Sunderland he was a passionate bibliophile.
He knew Europe well and spoke French more fluently than
any other courtier. Sophisticated, adroit, elegant, he was
very welcome at Court; like Sunderland he had been born
on the inside. He was, however, a very kindly man, not disposed to quarrel and preferring peace and harmony. So
for a time he stood aside from all groups and listened to
their fears and anxieties, and even sympathised with them,
a practice which as the months passed he carried to the
point of duplicity.

George I, naturally enough, was eager to visit Hanover.
After all, the first fifty-four years of his life had been spent
there. As Elector of Hanover he possessed far greater
powers over his subjects than in England, and it was highly
inconvenient to rule at a distance, in an age when posts
were slow and dilatory. The Jacobite rebellion and its
aftermath had kept him in England far longer than he
had intended. Before the King left his country in July
1716,[8] he had to settle what was for him a most distasteful
problem—what powers the Prince of Wales should enjoy
during his absence. The King would have preferred none,

[8] The clause in the Act of Settlement which forbade the monarch
to leave the country without the consent of Parliament was unani-
mously repealed.

but business had to go forward and signatures were required for documents. The King, however, refused to make him Regent and instead some quick-witted adviser dug out the title *Guardian of the Realm and Lieutenant*, which had not been in use since the time of the Black Prince. To this primary insult was added a host of others. No decision whatsoever was to be made by the Prince on any question touching foreign affairs. No vacancy could be filled by him in the Royal Household, Treasury and Admiralty, nor could he make a Governor of a garrison, nor promote above a colonel, nor even make a lieutenant in the Guards. Indeed the Prince was rendered powerless and the fact widely published. To rub a little salt in the wound the King dismissed the Prince's closest friends, Argyll and his brother, from their posts and then departed for Hanover, taking Stanhope with him.

The next few months passed in a welter of intrigue and mounting frustration in London if not in Hanover. Sunderland, immediately the King departed, developed a diplomatic illness, and secured permission to go to Aix for his health. Aix quickly changed to Hanover. Sunderland knew where power lay and he was acutely unhappy to be out of earshot of the Court. Stanhope made him welcome. Townshend and Walpole were now caught between the devil and the deep blue sea. They had to go to Hampton Court to the Prince and it was immediately repeated to Hanover that they were intriguing against the King and inciting the Prince to seize power. Argyll and his brother did their best to foment mischief and taught the Prince to regard Townshend and Walpole as the King's spies. This made business intolerably difficult, but as they improved their position with the Prince they lost ground at Hanover, where Sunderland was busy misinterpreting their every move. A nightmare quality was added to this situation by the fact that the King in Hanover had entered on a series of involved and delicate negotiations with the French and with the Baltic powers. The inevitable delays—contrary winds held up the Channel packets for days—drove the King frantic. Townshend and Walpole feared that British interests would be sacrificed for the sake of an arrangement which would merely gratify Hanover. This made them cautious, hesitant, prone to delay and, in the end, insistent that the King should return from Hanover or that the Prince should summon a meeting of Parliament. Both suggestions made the King choleric. The final upshot was that the King's return was heralded by Townshend's removal from his post—news conveyed to him somewhat coldly by Stanhope. Much to Walpole's and Townshend's chagrin they learnt that this sympathetic friend to whom they had poured out their fears and anxieties was in the pocket of Sunderland. In dudgeon Townshend and Walpole went into opposition and the brief harmony created by the accession and the rebellion was over. Furthermore a pattern of domestic politics was established which was to last throughout the reigns of the first four Georges.

4

Although there were two parties—Whigs and Tories—and every man in politics tended to have this primary label, yet no party was ever unified, and after 1717 there were always some Whigs in opposition. This was largely the reverse of what happened in Queen Anne's reign, when the Tory party had been far more disjointed than the Whigs and most Tory ministries had had some Tory groups in opposition to them. Also in 1717 it was quite on the cards that the Tories might get back into the King's favour. Not all Tories were tainted with Jacobitism, and in any case the taint was not at all difficult to remove. And the Germans rather favoured the idea of encouraging the Tories, on the simple principle that the more competing groups there were, the easier it would be for them to hold the balance of power. So in 1717, after the departure of Townshend and Walpole from the ministry, it looked to most knowledgeable men that the politics of Hanoverian England were to run very much as they had done in the time of Anne. They were mistaken. Although the Whigs were never again to know unity, the Tories were never to achieve place until the reign of George I's great-grandson.

In Queen Anne's reign Whig and Tory opposition groups had rarely worked closely together. Townshend and Walpole changed all that. Once they had quitted the ministry they were hardly distinguishable from the Tories with whom they associated. They attacked dissenters and toleration; pleaded for mercy to Oxford and Jacobites; savaged the King's foreign policy; bellowed against Hanover, Germans, and corruption. They made maximum nuisances of themselves, no matter if they flatly contradicted themselves, and never considered the consequences. Disgruntled Whigs, out of office, were to adopt the same tactics time and time again throughout the eighteenth century. Such a proceeding gives an air of unreality, almost of hypocrisy, to Hanoverian politics—the more so because it is difficult to disentangle them from our own fundamental concepts of political behaviour.

Townshend and Walpole could not put their differences of opinion to the people to be voted on. George I chose his ministers, elections took place when Parliament had run its course. The only way for them to get back into power was by hindering the King's business so intolerably that he would take them back in order to render secure the necessary business of government—the voting of supplies and the approval of foreign policy. Such a forcing bid was desperately difficult to bring off. Chatham managed it; so did Rockingham; both were helped by national disasters of considerable magnitude. Making a nuisance of oneself was too speculative a policy to pursue single-mindedly, and it was best combined with back-stairs intrigues. Harley had been a master of this process and illustrated with Mrs. Masham the way such matters should be conducted. The obvious channels for Walpole and Townshend were the King's mistresses and their mutual jealousies, so that at the same time as these politicians were fulminating against the King's government they were always prepared, and indeed frequently engaged, in letting the Court know their price.

Such a system could flourish partly because there was no real clash of conflicting political systems. Legislation in our sense was rare. Parliament only met for a few months in the year and then it was largely engaged on voting supplies and passing private bills. The aim of politics was not directed to liberties—they had been won in 1688—nor to social justice, but to the pursuit of office. Those who obtained power might do their utmost to rule in what they considered the best interests of the nation. Those permanently out of office might support or oppose them according to their consciences, but those seeking office or recently cast from it opposed not so much from principle but in order to make themselves nuisances. Townshend and Walpole were the first politicians to adopt consistently and blatantly such a policy, which later became almost conventional. Great events or large issues could and did arise, particularly later in the century, which were too grave for men to settle purely in terms of a personal search for power. Nevertheless, such is the duplicity of the human heart and the ingenuity of the human head that it is remarkable how frequently conscience and ambition were harmoniously combined. 1717, however, remains a date of major importance for Georgian politics—the first battle of the " ins " and the " outs " in which the " outs " adopt the traditional policies of the Tories. This year also witnessed the emergence of another recurring theme of Georgian political life—a quarrel between the King and Prince of Wales, a quarrel of momentous proportions.

George I returned, suspicious and bad-tempered, from Hanover in March 1717. He hated leaving his palace at Herrenhausen. He believed that the Prince had attempted with some success to ingratiate himself with the English people at the expense of the King's reputation. The Prince had aped the ruler in his father's lifetime—an act always intolerably irritating to monarchs. When they met, they were scarcely civil to each other. The final explosion occurred in November 1717 through a situation that was both farcical and typically Hanoverian. The Princess of Wales gave birth to a baby boy. The Prince wished to name its godparents, the King insisted on the protocol, named them himself, and included, again, according to the protocol, his Chamberlain, the Duke of Newcastle, whom the Prince detested. At the ceremony the Prince failed to control his feelings, took Newcastle by the elbow and said, " Rascal, I find you out." Newcastle was easily put in a twitter, and this mark of royal displeasure, combined with the Prince's rather strong accent, put him in such a dither that he thought the Prince had said, " I'll fight you." Appalled and confused he rushed to consult his colleagues, even disturbing Sunderland at his daughter's wedding. They advised him to go to the King, so he did, and told him that he had been challenged. The King immediately placed the Prince under what was virtually house arrest—without bothering to ask him for his version of the story. The hatred which the King felt for his son, and which was returned in good measure, was at last open and avowed. The Court had never known such drama and the whole of London was agog with excitement. After all, Königsmarck and Dorothy had given George I something of a sinister reputation.

The King called a cabinet, and the rumour ran that he told his ministers that had he been in Hanover he would have known perfectly well what to have done with the Prince, but being in England he wished to conform to the laws. Naturally the cabinet suggested negotiation and emissaries went to and fro; the Prince, somewhat unnerved, wrote letters full of respect, couched in very submissive terms. They received no reply. After four days the cabinet remembered the Habeas Corpus Act, by which no one could be detained without cause being shown, and suggested to the King that the continued detention of the Prince at St. James's might be regarded as a breach of the law. The King, therefore, expelled the Prince; the Princess followed. The King let it be known that anyone paying his court to the Prince and Princess would not be regarded as a friend of his. He also seized their children, secured a decision from the judges that he had the right to control their education, rapped the Prince and Princess over the knuckles for visiting their children secretly, and rationed them to one visit a week so long as notice was given to him first. The Prince decided to stay away.

The exiles took Leicester House and it quickly became the centre of the opposition's social life—gayer, livelier and much more ebullient than the Court. After all, the King was fifty-seven and punished his body in more ways than one. The future was bound to belong to the Prince. Politicians out of place could indulge in fantasies of power

to come. Naturally Townshend and Walpole soon found
their way to Leicester House. The Prince quickly got over
his dislike of them, the Princess found their inexhaustible
political speculation entrancing. Walpole particularly was
prepared to spend hours with her discussing the tactics by
which the King's government could be most completely
embarrassed. His eye was very much on the future. In
1718 too, the Prince's opposition had an air of novelty—
something as fresh and as startling in English political life
as Townshend and Walpole's outright opposition. As with
the latter it was soon to become a commonplace. Twenty
years later the Prince's own son had established himself at
Leicester House to be a thorn in his father's side. When
he died suddenly, his wife maintained the tradition. And
George III had the same trouble as soon as his son was old
enough to make mischief. The Georges did not like their
heirs and certainly their heirs did not like their father.
And this dislike, although hatred would be the juster
word, had curious repercussions on English political life.

An heir in conflict with the King gave added spice to
political life and greater unity and reality to an opposition.
For one thing the Prince disposed of a considerable amount
of private patronage—and also, as Duke of Cornwall, he
could influence a number of parliamentary elections.
Hence opposition need not be so arid to the politician if
the Prince favoured him. He might have a place, a fairly
safe seat in Parliament and excellent prospects for the
future when the Prince succeeded. Naturally the Prince's
Court tended to attract young men who either had little
hope of forcing their way into the settled pattern of a
governing faction, or wished to gamble for high stakes by
capturing the Prince's regard. Usually then, the Prince's
court was livelier, brighter, younger, more full of fun of
every variety; the satire and wit and gossip sharper and

more entrancing. In any case the Prince's Court provided
a focus which otherwise the opposition tended to lack.
There can be little doubt that throughout the eighteenth
century oppositions were more effective and much more
dangerous to the ministry when a Prince was in conflict
with his father. On the other hand, when there was no
Prince or when he was an infant, or not at loggerheads
with the King, the opposition was forced, as we shall see,
on to a different tack. Then they had to spend much more
time in rousing public opinion. and in attempting to create
great issues by dexterous propaganda. In 1718 the
quarrel between George I and the Prince of Wales created
a situation much to the advantage of Townshend and Walpole—a fact which they quickly realised and exploited
with great skill.

The quarrel with the Prince may have had one other
startling result—this time on the development of the
constitution. Queen Anne had presided at her cabinet
councils—usually held after dinner on Sundays—and King
George had continued the practice on his accession to the
throne. The Prince of Wales had sat in council with his
father—because he was heir and because he understood
English. Most of the King's ministers understood and
spoke French (the King's usual language; he spoke and
wrote in it more commonly than in his native tongue), but
some did not, notably his Lord Chancellor, Cowper. All
state-papers were duplicated in French, too, which made
things easier, but it is unlikely that all cabinet business and
discussion took place in French, and the Prince's knowledge of English must have been very valuable to his father
—after all he could catch the *nuances* and follow the
quick interchanges in discussion and inform the King
afterwards. When the King had visited Hanover, the
Prince had presided over the cabinet meetings and con-

ducted the business in his father's name. So when the quarrel came, the King was in a quandary. The Prince was a regular member of the cabinet yet the King wished neither to speak to him nor to see him. Without the Prince's presence—and of course he could have been forbidden to attend—the proceedings became more boring and more incomprehensible to the King. Naturally neither Sunderland nor Stanhope wanted the Prince to be present at cabinet meetings, for that would have meant that Walpole and Townshend would receive advance knowledge of all that they intended and also be aware of the differences of opinion which were bound to arise amongst ministers. Since the death of William III, the bulk of the work of the cabinet had been done by the ministers, meeting together without the sovereign, as Lords of the Committee. So to escape from an embarrassing situation the King ceased to attend cabinets, except those which had purely formal business such as the pardon of criminals or the reading of his speech before the opening of Parliament. The Lords of the Committee became the effective cabinet, meeting without the King. The King then saw his chief ministers privately in his closet and agreed or disagreed with what they had done. This both circumvented the Prince and saved the King hours of tedium. It also perhaps placed a little more power in the hands of his ministers—not much, however, because the King's consent was needed for every act which they took, and private consultations enabled him to consult more closely with his German advisers, particularly on foreign affairs. However, the absence of the monarch from the cabinet—which is regarded as a most important development of the constitution—was due more to the propensity of the Hanoverians to quarrel with their heirs than to the King's ignorance of the English language.

6

A sense of security, the death of the old party leaders, the possession of Hanover and of an adult heir, these factors had given rise to a pattern of political and court life in the first years of George I's reign which was to recur again and again. The pursuit of office and the hope of gain had dissolved the ties of political principle which had bound men of the same party together or intensified into critical issues those differences of opinion on policy which are bound to arise at all times even in the most harmonious ministries. The conflict of opinion between the leaders of the Whig party could easily have been resolved or accommodated had there been even a modicum of goodwill on either side. There was none.

The strife of faction went on for three years; at first Walpole gained ground and made Stanhope and Sunderland very uneasy; an attempt was made to detach Walpole from his friends. He refused to be won over and stayed in opposition. The ministry's hold over the Commons remained precarious—on the Peerage Bill in 1719 they were signally defeated—nevertheless they held their own. After a year or two they, too, began to get at cross-purposes with the German mistresses and advisers who, naturally enough, began to discover virtues in Walpole and Townshend that they had hitherto ignored, and Stanhope and Sunderland began to fear that they might easily change places with Walpole and Townshend unless they got ahead of the Germans. Accordingly they opened direct negotiations with the opposition and kept the Germans in ignorance of it—the advisers at least, if not the mistresses.

Walpole and Townshend were willing to throw in their hand if they could get easy terms. Walpole could not afford the luxury of a too prolonged opposition and the success of the ministry's financial venture with the South Sea Company had added to its prestige and strength. The future looked black to the two brothers-in-law. However, the ministry insisted that the King and Prince should be reunited; the Prince commanded too much influence in the House of Commons for the ministry's comfort and they wanted greater margins of security in both Houses. It did not prove an easy task to secure a truce in the Royal Family's feud. Walpole had become immensely friendly with the Princess of Wales. Like spoke to like. In physique and temperament they were two leaves from the same twig. Almost instinctively they began to work together, delighted to discover the same taste for power, the same enjoyment in the art of management. In the next reign this alliance was to achieve formidable proportions and to stamp both Court and politics with its own strange quality. Its first victory was won in 1720; Caroline got her husband down on his knees before the King—almost without conditions. The one which he insisted on—that he should not live at St. James's—was a matter upon which the King was only too eager to comply. Reconciled he might be with his son, yet he preferred to set eyes on him as little as possible. The Hanoverians had an astonishing capacity to act with utter gracelessness and the reconciliation of the King and Prince was one of their more outstanding performances. The King choked with rage at the sight of the embarrassed, kneeling, red-faced Prince. His eyes blazed with fury and all that he could struggle to say was "*Votre conduite . . . Votre conduite*" before turning abruptly and leaving the Prince. The next day at Chapel

the King completely ignored the Prince's presence. Sheer
hatred of his own offspring seems to have been one of the
more powerful emotions experienced by George I. Naked
though the feelings of the King and Prince might be, yet
they were honest; a marked contrast to those of their
ministers. They were to be seen about the Court with
their arms about each others' necks, laughing and joking.
Off they went to dinner together, drank each other supine
with toasts to friendship and unity. These jollifications
took place in June and early July. The King then took
himself off with his mistresses to Hanover, the Prince's
hands tied as stringently as ever. Suddenly the scene darkened; the South Sea Bubble blew up and burst—an event
of profound consequence for the Court and for the development of English politics.

Basically the English economy was exceptionally sound.
There was a growing favourable trade balance which
stimulated agriculture, industry, and commerce. The financial structure on the other hand was largely experimental
and frequently chaotic. There were sound institutions—
the Bank of England and the great chartered corporations
—but there was little control of credit. Many men felt
that the great credit resources of the state had not been
properly developed and that if they were, great prosperity
would ensue. Arguments such as these had enabled John
Law to launch his great financial experiment of the Mississippi Company in France. Similar ideas were in the minds
of the directors of the South Sea Company. This Company
had little to do with the South Seas; its monopoly of trade
to these regions was never expected to bring quick riches,
and it was largely a credit boost. The Company's main
function was financial, a counterpart or even rival of the
Bank of England, and the intention was for it to take over a
large segment of the national debt at a fixed interest and to

use its credit to finance capital expansion. Unfortunately this was not the whole story; the directors, or many of them and the most influential, wanted to get rich very quickly. They ignored the most obvious financial safeguards. They bribed politicians with stock; the King's mistresses, too; and even the King himself became a large stock-holder. Deplorable methods were used to inflate stock prices to make quick capital gains. The situation got out of hand. The country had recovered from the dislocation caused by the outbreak of peace in 1713; there was a lot of money about and gambling was the wine of life to many men and women. Speculation gripped London like the plague; companies both sensible and bogus sprouted like fungi. The inevitable crash came and shook the very foundations of government. The enraged victims, many bankrupt and destitute, demanded justice and revenge. So ugly, so dangerous, was the situation that George I, enjoying the autumnal delights of Herrenhausen, was rudely disturbed and forced to return to his turbulent and distracted Kingdom with two thoughtful and worried mistresses.

"There never was such distraction and undoing in any country," wrote Colonel William Windham to his brother in Norfolk on 27 September 1720. "You can't suppose the number of families undone. One may say almost everybody is ruined who has traded beyond their stock. Many a 100,000 men not with a groat and it grieves me to think of some of them."[4] Very few had been as wise as old Thomas Guy or Sarah Marlborough who had got away on the top of the market. Fewer had been luckier than Walpole, who had been saved from a thumping loss by a delay in the post and the wisdom of his banker. Most ministers were in a state of abject terror and anxiety. The shady

[4] *Felbrigg mss.*

dealings which had offered such easy, golden prospects now darkened their consciences. The independent country gentlemen and the opposition, however, were out for blood. They had been bamboozled and, come what may, chaos or Stuarts, they wanted revenge.

At this point Robert Walpole stepped forward. Twelve months later the King was as secure as ever on his throne; the Whig party as powerful as it had ever been since 1714; and Robert Walpole himself well on the way to a new and loftier eminence. This was achieved by political success, not by financial genius. The measures by which Walpole hoped to clear up the mess of the South Sea Bubble were never put in operation. The economic condition of the country was so buoyant that it quickly recovered once confidence was restored. Walpole's success lay in his defence of the Court and his colleagues against those who thirsted for justice and revenge. This was not easy; angry men wished for scapegoats. Walpole had to sacrifice one or two minor politicians—and fortunately for him death also came to his aid. One Craggs committed suicide, the other dropped dead. Stanhope, who was sharply attacked, had apoplexy. Nevertheless Walpole screened Sunderland and prevented an enquiry reaching the Court. When the crisis was over he had placed himself in an extremely strong position. To save the King and his mistresses he had withstood violent criticism and abuse; and so the King had incurred obligations to him and to Townshend. The mortality of their enemies also increased their political eminence. They were still, however, far from possessing a position of absolute authority. Sunderland's hatred of them had not been lessened by being obliged to them. He had plenty of friends and allies at Court and in the ministry. He was a sufficiently supple politician to look to an alliance with Bolingbroke and any other willing Tory with equanimity. Had he lived, Sunderland and not Walpole might have dominated the next twenty years of political life. He dropped dead on 22 April 1722 and Walpole and Townshend found themselves in an almost unassailable position which they proceeded to exploit. They created a system which became the envy of future generations and made stable what had never been stable before—parliamentary monarchy.

7

They began by systematically destroying their rivals. In their places they promoted safe men on whom they could absolutely rely. They subjected the whole machinery of government to the closest scrutiny; every office which fell vacant—in the Church, in the Army, Navy, or Law, as well as in the departments of state and the King's Household, was given either to their relations and friends or to men whose loyalty their allies could guarantee. The Tories, whose hopes had risen during the South Sea crisis, were cast back into the wilderness by the thorough exploitation of a Jacobite Plot—Atterbury's. London, which became obstreperous, had its charter remodelled to increase the power of Walpole's friends. The Court was kept happy by generous provision for the Civil List, and there was no nearer way to George I's heart than through his pocket. This policy implacably applied and steadfastly pursued gave his ministry a commanding and unassailable majority in both Houses. The King's business was carried through without difficulty. The Court had not enjoyed so firm a control over Parliament since the days of the Tudors.

The creation of a strong political system, impervious to the blows of opposition, was not the only consideration of Townshend and Walpole. They were also statesmen. Townshend pursued peace and achieved it. Walpole, a formidably efficient man of business, made the administrative machine work. He was quickly responsive to any suggestion which might increase trade and prosperity and, once convinced, gave it the force of law. The success of their policies lulled criticism and drew into their orbit many fair-minded, independent men who were happy to support good government and low taxation, even though the perquisites of office were being ruthlessly exploited for the enrichment of a clique.

These years of peace and success in which the temperature of political life was consistently lowered gave a security to the Hanoverian succession which we take for granted, yet must have seemed far more problematic to contemporaries. When George I set out for Hanover for the last time in June 1727, he left behind him strong government and a reasonably contented people. To those who remembered, and there were many, the alarms and excursions of the previous generation, with its plots, rebellions, and civil wars in Scotland and Ireland, the change must have seemed almost miraculous. Fortune had been kind to George I; the Jacobites had failed to exploit a number of favourable opportunities. The interference and intrigues of his German advisers had been less disastrous and less resented than they might have been. His own predilections for English politicians—almost uniformly wrong-headed—had not borne the evil fruit for his people which they might so easily have done. Death corrected his mistakes; death whose prevalence and skittish nature we tend to ignore and leave out of account. When George I set out for Hanover in the summer of 1727 he was a hearty man of sixty-seven. His mother had lived to be eighty-four and, in spite of his self-indulgences, many must have thought, as Walpole devoutly hoped, that he would follow her example. Near Osnabrück he had a stroke and died, and the system which Walpole and Townshend had fought so hard to create was placed in jeopardy.

CHAPTER III

GEORGE II

1727—1760

Although Queen Caroline had developed a strong attachment to Walpole, George II had, from the time of the reconciliation, regarded him with a certain hostility. Walpole's enemies, therefore, whether secret or avowed, were jubilant and they confidently expected to witness and enjoy the humiliation of this arrogant statesman. Walpole informed the new king of George I's death in another of those farcical situations which seemed to dog the Hanoverians at moments of high drama. The Prince was at Richmond, and in bed with his wife, when the Duchess of Dorset informed him of Sir Robert's presence. Half-dressed, the King told him to go and take his orders from Spencer Compton; twenty-four hours later the Queen had circumvented this act of rash folly, and Sir Robert, who had expressed, not very convincingly, his willingness to occupy any subordinate position about the Court, was back in office, drawing up plans for an increased civil list and the discharge of the royal debts. Walpole knew well enough that favour demanded favours. Indeed the impossibility of anyone else's getting the money from Parliament had been Caroline's strongest card in making her husband eat his words. This somewhat ludicrous accession crisis was symbolic of the first ten years of George II's reign and illustrates the true disposition of power at Court. Caroline ruled her husband and she was devoted to Sir Robert. All three were remarkable, all odd personalities,

and the strong ties which bound them together were of
immense importance for the development of their country.
Had Walpole fallen, Bolingbroke was lurking in the
wings, and the mixed administrations which had so bedevilled the politics of Anne's reign, owing to the constant
shift of influence, might easily have started once more.
As it was, Walpole's system became stronger than ever;
however, the reason for that strength lay primarily in the
confidence which he enjoyed at Court, first with Caroline,
and afterwards with George II.

Like his father George was stupid but complicated. He
had certain obvious gifts. He had an excellent memory,
very exact and precise, which he enjoyed exercising in a
number of ways. He possessed a formidable knowledge
of the genealogy of the European nobility and of the
uniforms and accoutrements of all the regiments of
Europe. His passion for dates and data led him to be quite
well versed in history, which he read with enjoyment.
Unlike his father he was not indolent; business came quite
easily to him. At Raynham in Norfolk, the seat of Lord
Townshend, there is a great pile of notes of George II, all
in his own hand, stretching over the first three years of his
reign—comments on despatches and reports of Townshend
and his ambassadors abroad. All the comments are terse,
very much to the point, and not infrequently shrewd.[1]
Yet George II lacked confidence; whether the miseries of
his mother or the bullying, alternating with neglect, of his
father created a deep sense of uncertainty is a matter for
speculation. Maybe it was just a part of his environment.
Nevertheless the effect for English history was important.
George II could be bullied. Caroline was a mistress of the
art; his ministers, after her death, quickly learnt the trick.

[1] A small selection of these was published by W. Coxe in his *Life
and Administration of Sir Robert Walpole*, II, 520-41.

Knowing that he would give way, and hating the knowledge, at times put him into fierce, semi-hysterical rages. The obstinacy, which was such a part of the Hanoverian temperament, often prevented him from yielding easily or gracefully. Undignified scenes were a part and parcel of his weakness.

The same uncertainty infused his sexual relations. His father possessed a coarse, animal appetite, eager for satisfaction, and not over-delicate as to how it was gratified. True he developed habits and remained loyal after his fashion to the Duchess of Kendal and Kielmannsegge. His son was capable of flirtation.[2] Lady Cowper thought that he slept with Walpole's wife (not that Walpole would have minded; he and his wife were on very easy terms); and there is gossip of other casual relationships, though they never seriously engaged his attention. His preference obviously lay towards regular and methodical relationships and his mistresses usually lasted a very long time. When he came to the throne Mrs. Henrietta Howard had enjoyed his favours for the best part of ten years. She was nearly as plain as the late King's mistresses and also unfortunately rather deaf. She was a friend of Pope, Gay, and to a lesser extent Bolingbroke, who, after his pardon in 1725, hoped through her to gain the King's ear. A modest, discreet, rather witty woman, she seems to have made no attempt to play politics, or to have been checked if the attempt was made. Most evenings the King, who liked to parade his gallantry, would go to her apartments at nine o'clock precisely—often waiting for the hour to strike, pacing up and down the drawing-room, watch in hand.

And yet George II was deeply in love with his wife.

---

[2] His approaches were no more delicate than his father's. Smitten by the very pretty but reluctant Mary Bellenden—a Maid of Honour to the Princess—he sat by her and counted the gold in his purse not once but twice until the girl fled from the room.

Although Caroline grew quite fat, she remained comely, possessing a lovely pink and white skin and beautiful flaxen hair. Short in stature, nevertheless she gave the impression of force and intelligence. She, too, had a streak of coarseness; or perhaps one might call it a frank interest in sexual activity. (She once cross-questioned Lord Hervey extensively about the capacity of her son for fatherhood.) And there can be little doubt that both she and the King thoroughly enjoyed their marriage bed. When the King became infatuated at Hanover in 1735 with the Countess von Walmoden, he wrote long letters to Caroline, describing in exact detail each stage of his conquest. On his return he could hardly wait until he had taken Caroline into his arms, thereby giving rise to considerable ribaldry amongst his courtiers. She herself did everything possible to conceal the rupture of her womb from which she died, fearing that the knowledge of it might displease the King and drive him from her arms. Odd, certainly, both of them were, rather nerveless in their tastes, not particularly happy with each other's temperament, yet bound together in passion, knitted together by the lusts of their flesh. The disparity of their characters misled all but the most perceptive into thinking that the King might be most easily approached through his mistresses, until Sir Robert Walpole demonstrated to the Court that Caroline was mistress as well as Queen, or, as he bluntly put it in the coarse, rustic way which he affected, "He took the right sow by the ear."

Until she died George trusted his wife and depended on her judgement. But for their fundamental adjustment to each other both might easily have found life intolerable. George II was an exceedingly impatient man, who needed life to proceed with meticulous regularity. Each Saturday he thundered off to Richmond with his cavalcade of pre-

cisely dressed officers. Meals were regular and to the
moment. He hated the unexpected, and any breaking of
his routine fretted him like acid on the skin. Though he
liked the company of clever women, nevertheless they were
bored to exhaustion by the tedium of his presence and the
fret of his restlessness. His one delight, which at least his
wife could share, was his passion for music and for opera;
it is due as much to George II as to anyone that Handel
secured the encouragement which led him to make his
home in England. He had no use for the other arts and
graces which adorn the life of man. His only other pre-
occupations, apart from music, were his guards and his
money. His guards he tended with loving care. A brave
man, he was only too eager to lead them into battle. His
attachment to them was strengthened by his envy of his
brother-in-law Frederick of Prussia's magnificent army.
Owing to the Englishman's hatred of standing armies he
could never hope to compete with Frederick, with the consequence that his detestation of him, which grew year by
year, was not without its influence on British foreign
policy.

His wife, on the other hand, was a woman of singular
accomplishment. She had been a friend of Leibniz and her
knowledge of philosophy was considerable. Her chief
interest lay in theological speculation, in which she leaned
towards deism and the rationalist approach to the universe,
which was rapidly becoming popular, yet she also had sympathy with the mystical side of religion and proved a toler-
ant friend, and at times an influential patron, of Tories
inclining to high church views. Indeed church patronage
was the one subject upon which she and Sir Robert Walpole did not always see eye to eye; and on occasion they
almost quarrelled about the appointment of bishops—a
vital question for Sir Robert, as a bishop commanded a

vote in the House of Lords. Usually they responded to each other like two harmonious instruments of music. Intelligent, coarse-fibred, full of appetite for life, they were both of an age at which the delights of power tasted ever sweeter with the passing years. Furthermore, their strength was so great that they grew to resent with all the bitterness and fury of their natures the slightest attack on their greatness. They hated the challenge of men of ability; disliked criticism; enjoyed sycophancy and thought it truth. Gradually, as they destroyed those friends and allies who were proud enough to maintain an attitude of independence, they reached a lonely and dangerous eminence. Yet never again until William Pitt the Younger became George III's minister was a government so secure, so certain of its authority as Sir Robert Walpole's during those early years of George II's reign, and it is time to take a closer look at this singular man and to assess his influence on the development of Hanoverian England.

2

Walpole was a short, dumpy man, weighing rather more than twenty stone. His arms and legs were short; his heavy head sprang almost straight from his shoulders. His features were large and coarse—square double chin, strongly marked black eyebrows, straight, thinnish mouth, with a thick, protruding underlip, a sharp emphatic nose. Yet about the face there were the undeniable marks of humour and intelligence which gave these strong features both animation and charm. The bright brown eyes and the mobile mouth whose corners seem almost to twitch in his most formal and wooden portraits rescued the face from the commonplace. The wide-spaced eyes gave him an air of surprised frankness, an openness that was curiously engaging and highly deceptive. As blunt and as outspoken as any man when he wished to be, yet he could be as supple and as subtle as a serpent. Above all he exuded power, an aspect of his character so obvious that many were disturbed by it, fearing and resenting his certainty, his desire for personal control. A character of such complexity, he had, throughout his life, been either loved or hated; sometimes both, but few, except perhaps his mother—a curiously opaque character—had been indifferent to him. Now in the noonday of his power he was the most sought-after man in the kingdom, the most feared, the most detested, and against him there was a snarling outcry of impotent rage.

Walpole, however, was not merely a royal favourite, although he was that, and derived much strength from such a position; he also possessed great positive qualities which made him even more formidable. He was the first King's servant to refuse a peerage and to stay in the House of Commons. At first this had been done very largely for tactical reasons. His success in mastering difficulties—particularly the South Sea Bubble—and the obvious inconveniences experienced by his enemies in the House of Lords, brought the realisation that the best place for a King's minister was in the Commons, for there the power of the Crown—owing to a large and important body of independents—was always more problematic than in the Lords, where the bishops and courtiers could be expected to give the King his majority.

In the Commons Walpole had his corner where his cronies gathered—his little army of placemen, civil servants, and friends which he marshalled like a general for the great debates. They provided the core of his strength. However, by themselves they were probably never quite sufficient to give him more than the barest of majorities. For security he needed to sway men who sat in the corners most distant from the Speaker's chair or who hid themselves modestly on back-benches. These were the country squires, the men who came to Westminster for honour's sake, because they stood well in their own neighbourhood or belonged to families who had sent their sons to Westminster for time out of mind. They rarely spoke, and in times without stress were not, perhaps, over-energetic in their attendance, coming up late for the session in January, unless hard weather had curtailed their hunting and shooting, and disappearing early as soon as the Easter recess loomed on the horizon. They could, however, be roused. They knew their neighbourhoods and were responsive to the opinions voiced by their brother justices of the peace; and their somnolence could quickly turn, as it had done during the South Sea Bubble, into an excited interest in politics. These men Walpole cultivated and it was partly for their sakes that he went on sitting in the Commons. He enjoyed, of course, very much the cut and thrust of debate, and no one took a greater delight than he in the details of business, but he felt safer if he had the country gentlemen under his own eye.

For them he cultivated a deliberate rusticity, and parodied the Norfolk squire. The gossip, much encouraged, ran that he always opened his game-keeper's letters before his despatches. He had a trick of munching little red Norfolk apples to sustain him during the debates. His language in private was as coarse as any squire's; in debate so simple and direct that even the stupidest could follow him. His letters possess the same plain, matter-of-fact quality. Like his oratory they were free from tropes, similes, metaphors. All of this was a deliberate part of his public character. Fortunately for Walpole—and, of course, he

would never have convinced had it not been so—this
persona had its roots in his own temperament. In spite of
his bulk he was an active, muscular man with a genuine
passion for hunting. He loved his hounds and enjoyed his
Saturday afternoons chasing the stag in Richmond Park,
of which he acted as Ranger.[8] There, too, he kept his
mistress—Molly Skerrett. Walpole made no attempt at
concealment. All the world knew that he and his wife had
long ceased to have any use for each other. There was
nothing pretentious about Molly. She came from compara-
tively humble circumstances. Her wit and charm rather
than her beauty conquered Walpole. The Queen professed
to be at a loss how such a pleasant girl could sleep with
anyone so grossly fat as Walpole. Neither Walpole nor
Molly Skerrett, however, were as obsessed by the appetites
of the flesh as the Queen. Although Walpole had from
time to time made a parade of his gallantry, his interest in
women was far less specific. He wanted the security of
love and the knowledge of devotion. And Molly gave him
the affectionate and intelligent companionhip which his
passionate and hysterical wife had failed to provide.

The honesty, the plainness, the directness of his manner,
both private and public, attracted many country squires
who were suspicious of sophistication, of the affected
elegancies of many courtiers. His avowed lechery and his
periodic carousals appealed to the earthy side of their
natures. At the same time, of course, these habits annoyed
those aristocratic circles who were deeply concerned with
questions of breeding. Hervey and Chesterfield constantly
comment with superiority and disdain on the grossness of
Walpole's manners. The King's personal friends—Scarborough, Spencer Compton and the rest—never liked him;

---

[8] The office of Ranger belonged to his son, Robert Lord Walpole;
Walpole acted as his deputy.

they felt him to be an outsider, a man who had got beyond himself.

They felt this much more keenly because, although he preserved and enjoyed the rustic habits of a Norfolk squire, just as he kept his Norfolk accent, he did not live like one; on the contrary, few aristocrats could vie with him in the profusion of his expenditure. He lived in grandeur. He built Houghton, a splendid small palace for which the furniture and the pictures were bought without any consideration of the cost; Rubenses, Rembrandts, Vandycks and Poussins were purchased at record prices. At Chelsea, at Richmond, at Arlington Street, the pictures and the furniture were of the same high standard. He lived high—often spending over a thousand a year on wine —and his generosity was richly profuse. Coarse and brutal he might be in many of his ways, but he loved with all the richness of his nature the beauty of adornment. His taste was more unerring and more confident than most of the simpering, theorising aesthetes who created the world of fashion. Of course it was very unwise of him to live in such ostentatious grandeur, and many thought him a hypocrite. Some thought the rustic squire a pretence to catch votes, others regarded his aristocratic splendour as a show to dazzle the Court and make men place-hungry. Both were a part of his nature—he was as frank and as direct in his pride of wealth as in his speech.

His frankness and his directness bred other dangers. He had a true sense of family and a hard core of loyalty to those who had been unquestioningly loyal to him. He believed in rewards, in concrete rewards in the shape of places. He was the power in the land; his friends expected a good turn from him and he had every intention of fulfilling their expectations. As one turns over the directories of the Court officers his friends and relatives everywhere abound. Thomas Cremer, a Lynn merchant who had once lent him money, turns up at the Treasury in a minor office, but a comfortable sinecure. His Norfolk doctor—Hepburn—became Surgeon of Chelsea Hospital: his banger and cousin, Robert Mann, Collector of the Customs of the Port of London. One London newspaper listed in fury and bitterness the offices held by himself and his near relatives from 1722.

> First Lord of the Treasury, Mr. Walpole. Chancellor of the Exchequer, Mr. Walpole. Clerk of the Pells, Mr. Walpole's son. Customs of London, second son of Mr. Walpole, in Reversion.[4] Secretary of the Treasury, Mr. Walpole's brother. Postmaster-General, Mr. Walpole's brother. Secretary to Ireland, Mr. Walpole's brother. Secretary to the Postmaster-General, Mr. Walpole's brother-in-law.[5]

Only Walpole was surprised and infuriated when his ministry was labelled the "Robinocracy" and constantly libelled. Places meant money and places meant power and, as the stream flowed ever more powerfully to his Norfolk friends and relatives, the resentment of other men grew stronger.

The interaction of Walpole's position and character brought into being a secret opposition at Court and an avowed opposition in the Commons, both resolved to bring about the destruction of his influence. This proved hard to encompass, for Walpole's policy, if not his methods, commanded much respect. He was an admirable administrator and made the cumbersome machinery of eighteenth-century government work more efficiently than it was ever to work again. His policy was exceedingly simple—the avoidance of war, the encouragement of trade, the reduc-

---

[4] i.e. after Robert Mann.
[5] *The Craftsman*, Collected Edition (1737), XI, 16.

tion of taxation, and, for the rest, *status quo*—no innovations. As he rightly said, "I am no saint, no Spartan, no reformer."

3

Walpole's monopoly of power presented a target for the opposition, but for the early years of George II's reign this opposition lacked a proper focus—the heir to the throne, Frederick, Prince of Wales, had been educated in Hanover and did not arrive in England until December 1728.[6] He was not allowed a separate establishment and he was kept very much in subjection. Naturally enough the opposition quickly cast an eye longingly in his direction, but for the time being he could give them no help, even if he had wished to do so. They were driven to other expedients. After the death of Sunderland, in 1722, Walpole had eliminated his rivals and promoted those men who were never likely to be a threat to his supremacy. Such a policy made enemies. The bitterest was William Pulteney; he had followed Walpole loyally into the wilderness and when his faction returned to the promised land he had naturally expected the office which his talents demanded. He did not get it. Walpole distrusted his character and was jealous of his ability. After hanging about the Court for a year or so, sometimes acting loyally with it, sometimes railing at it, Pulteney settled down to consistent enmity. About the same time—1725—Bolingbroke reappeared on the scene. Through his wife he had got at the Duchess of Kendal, possibly bribed her, but certainly he obtained a hearing with George I. For a time it looked as if Bolingbroke might be pardoned absolutely for his Jacobite ex-

[6] He was born 4 February 1707.

cesses. After a great effort Walpole stopped this. Boling-broke was allowed to return to England but not to take his seat in the House of Lords. Walpole at least kept him out of Court politics. By 1726 Bolingbroke realised, like Pulteney, that he had no future so long as Walpole remained the King's minister. They got together and drew up schemes for raising a whirlwind of opposition which was to blow Walpole out of office. One of the chief instruments was to be the rousing of public opinion by the publication of a lively, trenchant, outspoken newspaper, *The Craftsman*. No sooner had they got that launched than George I had apoplexy and died. They became some-what quiescent until they saw that Walpole was as much in power as ever and then they began in earnest.

They made politics immensely exciting. They attacked Walpole in *The Craftsman*, in pamphlets, in ballads; so popular did ministry-baiting become that theatre managers tumbled over themselves to put on wildly libellous plays.[7] Walpole was made to resemble every Royal favourite in history and his relations with the Queen were made to appear utterly scandalous. The dependence of the King on his wife provided an inexhaustible theme for squibs, cartoons, and mock advertisements. The satirisation of the Court and the government had never been so relentless, so extensive or so popular. Owing to the growth of charity schools and private educational establishments literacy was rapidly spreading, and a far greater proportion of the population, particularly London's, could enjoy vicariously the political battle. Everyone's enjoyment was greatly enhanced because Walpole took abuse very badly. He was incapable of ignoring it; he resented it bitterly and tried to

[7] There were, of course, some good plays—*The Beggar's Opera*, for example, and the early plays of Fielding: *Tom Thumb, The Historical Register*, etc.

parry it by hiring journalists and buying newspapers. Unfortunately his choice of writers was frequently lamentable, and the wits of the opposition made great sport of their feeble and platitudinous efforts to explain the opposition charges away.

The opposition, of course, was not content merely with journalism. Pulteney was a Member of Parliament and so were his associates, Sir William Wyndham and William Shippen, one the head of the Hanoverian Tories, the other of the Jacobites. Nor was Pulteney the only Whig in opposition. There were relics of Sunderland's faction, and more important, a number of wealthy London merchants who were strongly opposed to Walpole's pacifism. These diverse elements Pulteney and Bolingbroke welded together and made them act in concert. They exploited parliamentary procedure and made life as difficult as possible for Walpole. They were constantly calling for papers, demanding special committees of enquiry, and introducing bills against political corruption. Just as Walpole tried to gain the independents by posing as one of them, or, at least, as one in sympathy with them, and actively engaged in their interests, so the opposition tried to win over the country gentlemen by exposing the iniquities of the Court.

To public agitation and parliamentary opposition was added Court intrigue. After all, Bolingbroke and Pulteney had been in politics long enough to know that no minister ever fell unless he lost the confidence of the Sovereign. Kings still ruled in England in an active sense. George II had to be convinced that he could no longer go on with Walpole; and although great uncertainty might be created in the King's mind by public clamour and parliamentary difficulties, these things needed to be strengthened. Walpole had enough enemies at Court for the opposition to find channels. They made some foolish steps. They tried using Mrs. Howard, but this proved a total failure. They had better luck with some of the King's personal friends who had hoped to do far better for themselves at his accession than, in fact, they had done. Chesterfield and Spencer Compton were the principal links with the opposition. They were discreet, keeping their enmity to sarcasm and pin-pricking, waiting for a real crisis which they could exploit. And there was the Prince. No real success could be expected until he had a separate establishment which would provide a number of places for young and needy politicians, so the Prince became an object of intimate concern both for the Court and the opposition. Walpole wanted him kept in subjection; the opposition wanted him freed.

In 1727 when the opposition started in earnest Walpole held the trump cards; he controlled the Court and enjoyed an ample majority in Parliament. Nevertheless each passing year was bound to strengthen the opposition. Walpole was fifty-one; the King forty-four; the Prince twenty. The future must belong to the Prince. The fight might be arduous and prolonged but the chance of the opposition's winning through was always great enough to keep it at a high pitch year after year. The sense that the country supported it strongly doubtless helped to sustain it in its efforts.

Politics are not merely a matter of strategy or of influence. Policy—now so often ignored by historians—was always a matter of great moment in the Georgian world. When men came to vote in the lobbies, factions dissolved and two parties emerged, those who said "yes" and those who said "no". True, some refrained from voting and held themselves aloof from the critical contests, but on all the great issues there were two sides, two parties, even though some men slipped from one side to the other with bewildering rapidity. The opposition to Walpole had a policy, quite a simple one, and they put it squarely to the public.

Their view was that England's interests were being sacrificed for Hanover's. In diplomacy Germany came first, the commercial needs of Britain a poor second. What was worse, the English people were paying for German mercenaries, necessary perhaps for Hanover, but totally unnecessary for England. The money should either be saved, and taxation reduced, or spent on the navy; after all, England was a maritime nation; the commercial empires of France and Spain, England's natural enemies, who threatened her prosperity, should be seized, if and when the chance came. Certainly England should never tolerate the treatment which Walpole weakly accepted from Spain. He allowed, almost without protest, the mutilation of English seamen and the seizure of English vessels. And Walpole was a crook, bent on gratifying the least whim of the King, in order to fill the Court with his sycophantic relatives whose wolfish appetites for plunder were as great as his own. They pointed to his houses, pictures, jewelry and finery, and asked how a simple Norfolk squire came honestly by such riches. And as for his so-called financial skill—pure legerdemain, said Pulteney. With his Sinking Fund Walpole had bamboozled the public into thinking the nation's debts were being reduced; in fact they were being steadily increased. As for his taxation policy, that was designed purely to favour the rich. His main skill was in hiding the fact that ultimately his taxation was borne, as ever, by the landowner. Squires had been blessed by an occasional reduction—always short-lived—in the land tax, but really they were bearing the burden of an extravagant Court, a corrupt minister, and a costly foreign policy which was conducted not in British interests but solely to make the King easy about Hanover. Much of this was plausible and contained a grain of truth. And certainly it appeared sufficiently cogent to convince an ever-growing band of supporters. Bolingbroke, to give the opposition greater universality, developed a superficial political theory, based on the idea of a Patriot King who was to rule with the best men drawn from all factions. His books and pamphlets contained the sententious platitudes with which self-justifying politicians like to lard their speeches. For the rest of the century ministers and opposition speakers dipped into his works and paid lip service to his views. No one, certainly not successful opposition, ever thought of putting his ideas into practice. They gave, however, a fine moral note to the opposition's attack.

In the first years of George's reign Walpole was annoyed but never endangered by the opposition, yet, as the years passed, his majorities in the Commons steadily fell and the group of secret ill-wishers at Court grew larger. More and more he relied heavily on the Queen for support. He managed to remove his brother-in-law, Townshend, without weakening himself in 1730, but three years later the Excise crisis, in which the opposition raised the country against him, very nearly brought about his ruin. Those at Court who hated him thought the moment had come to get rid of him. With the King's support he mastered them, but in so doing greatly strengthened his enemies at a time when the Prince was beginning to bestir himself in politics.

4

At first Frederick Prince of Wales had been kept in the schoolroom, but his subjection could not be maintained for long. By 1733 he was in sympathetic contact with the opposition; by 1734 he was creating difficulties at Court by demanding marriage and a separate establishment. By 1735 his tactics were being sharpened by opposition leaders. He obtained his marriage—his bride was Augusta of Saxe-Gotha—but he spent his honeymoon with her under the sharp eyes of his quarrelsome mother and father at St. James's. Two years later, when the Princess was nearly in labour, he fled with her from St. James's and thereby started an appalling row with the King, much to the opposition's delight. He rented Leicester House, like his father before him, refused to be reconciled, and created a home for the opposition; indeed he dabbled in opposition politics until he died in 1751. His life was spent in irritating the King and his ministers; habits which, after his death, his wife maintained. Leicester House, until 1760, provided an alternative court, a refuge for dispossessed politicians, and it became increasingly hard for any minister to acquire the immense and stable power which Walpole had exercised, in 1737, for nearly fifteen years. Nor was the Prince's power negligible. He exercised considerable influence over the parliamentary elections in Cornwall, which was his Duchy, and, of course, he could offer future prospects to the young. They clustered around him so eagerly that Walpole dubbed his party the " Patriot Boys ".

The conflict in the royal family marked the beginning of Walpole's end, and as the quarrel with the Prince not only brought about Walpole's downfall but also helped to make

Chatham's reputation (for he was one of the really outstanding " patriot boys "), it is worth considering in closer
detail, especially as it illumines the strange natures of
Caroline and George II. For these critical years there exists
a magnificent source—the *Memoirs of John Lord Hervey*,[8]
the best court memoirs in English and very nearly of equal
quality to the justly famous Duc de St. Simon's. Of course
Hervey was prejudiced. He was effeminate, malicious,
sharply intelligent, and could never resist a cutting phrase
even if some truth had to be sacrificed. After being rapturously fond of the Prince, Hervey came to loathe him.
The Prince preferred the charms of Hervey's mistress—
Miss Vane—to Hervey's and so doubly mortified him.
Hence his attitude to the Prince was very biased. Nevertheless, Hervey was very fond of Caroline, and probably
not eager to show her in an adverse light, and where he
can be tested, his facts, if not his interpretations, are
usually proved accurate.

Hervey portrays a fantastic picture. Both the King and
his Queen grew to loathe and detest their son. " If I was
to see him in hell," said Caroline, " I should feel no more
for him than I should for any other rogue that ever went
there." However, the King scolded her for being too
partial to the Prince whom he regarded as " a monster and
the greatest villain that ever was born ".[9] On her death-
bed Caroline resolutely refused the requests of the Prince
to see her—she regarded his demand to do so as sheer
hypocrisy. Indeed she maintained that his sole reason for
wanting to see her was to avoid appearing as an undutiful
son in the eyes of the public. And when she thought that
the Prince might inherit her private property, she could
not rest until the Lord Chancellor had been sent for. He

---

[8] They were splendidly edited by R. R. Sedgwick in 3 vols. in 1931.
[9] Hervey, *Memoirs* (ed. Sedgwick), III, 812-3.

eased her mind by telling her there was no such risk.[10] By the side of this quarrel in the royal family that between George I and his son was trivial indeed.

The venom with which the King and Queen pursued the Prince after he had left St. James's was the subject of endless gossip and, naturally enough, aroused great sympathy with the public. The Prince's popularity, in its turn, lifted the spirits of the opposition and gave them renewed energy to attack Walpole, for the difficulties of the Prince could be convincingly laid at his door. Indeed, many of his colleagues, remembering the former royal quarrel, thought that he had acquiesced too easily in the King's punitive measures against the Prince. The gossip began to circulate that Walpole was losing his nerve, that his increasing years (he was sixty-one in 1737) made him frightened of the future and too eager to please the King. Such rumours corroded the loyalty of his friends as much as they excited the appetite of the " patriot boys " who saw the promised land of office drawing ever nearer. Their spirits were raised by two other events, the death of the Queen and the worsening relations with Spain.

The death of the Queen was gruesome, farcical, and very moving. Both she and the King played out their parts in keeping with their singular natures. The King could not tolerate sickness. It made him angry. For years the Queen had pretended to him that her ruptured womb was in no way serious and at the same time she concealed it from the rest of the world. It grew worse, turned malignant, and forced her in November 1737 to take to her bed. The King was beside himself with irritation, remorse, and tenderness. At times he could not bear the sight of her and shouted that she looked like a calf that was about to have its throat cut; at times he was reduced to tears by her ten-

[10] Hervey, *Memoirs* (ed. Sedgwick), III, 891-2.

derness for him. She begged him to marry again; choking
back his sobs he stammered, "*Non—j'aurai—des—maît-
resses*", to which she wearily replied, "*Ah! Mon Dieu!
cela n'empêche pas.*" For days he scarcely left her bedside,
and when she died his courtiers were amazed by the
obvious depth of his feeling.[11]

As the courtiers waited for her to die, their speculations
naturally dwelt on the future. They watched Sir Robert,
full of tears and anxiety, rush to the King's closet on his
sudden return from Norfolk. The Queen spoke to him and
commended him to the King. Walpole's grief was so
great that he could scarcely force his ungainly bulk up
from his knees. Would he survive? Yes, emphatically
yes, the Duke of Newcastle told Devonshire, who was over
in Ireland acting as Lord Lieutenant. He admitted that,
" This is the greatest blow that ever he received and goes
deeper than any I have ever known. But a concern for
his own honour, the good of the public, a regard for his
friends, and a desire to comply with the dying requests of
the Queen, have determined him to engage and go on."[12]

It was never the same. Sir Robert was ageing, and even
his friends began to watch him with a cool and calculating
eye. His influence with the King, though great, was weakened. Newcastle and Hardwicke suggested trying to govern the King through his favourite daughter, and Walpole
snapped at them coarsely : " Did they expect the King to
go to bed with Princess Caroline?" Realistically Walpole
pushed forward an old mistress of the King's, Lady Deloraine, and pressed the King to fetch his latest fancy,
Madame Walmoden, from Hanover. Such was his anxiety
that he urged the Princesses to use their influence with

---

[11] Hervey, III, 878-917. Hervey's description of the Queen's death
is a masterpiece; so strange, so true, and curiously compassionate.
[12] *Chatsworth* mss 26 Nov. 1737; Newcastle to Devonshire.

their father to get her over. She came and agreeably impressed the English court—not at all an easy thing to do.

" She has fine black eyes and brown hair, and very well shaped ", wrote Ashe Windham to his cousin, Lord Townshend, " not tall nor low, has no fine features, but very agreeable in the main. She appears like one that has been used to the courts of Princes. It is not doubted that she will soon have an apartment at Kensington." His guess was right, she was soon installed as the King's mistress. She did not, however, take Caroline's place, no one could. Nevertheless the Countess Walmoden retained the King's affections and stayed with him until he died.[18] She proved, however, unwilling or unable to prop the crumbling edifice of Walpole's power.

The Queen's death had taken place at a critical moment. It followed hard on the fracas of the Prince's withdrawing from St. James's and thereby encouraging the opposition with a greater hope of success. Worse still was the Spanish situation for Walpole. For many long years the relations between the Spanish *guardacostas* and the English merchants in the West Indies had been very bad. The English smuggled; the Spaniards seized and punished. Their depredations and occasional sadism were used to inflame public opinion. Walpole, clutching at peace as if his power depended on it, tried negotiations which the Spaniards made long, laborious, and inconclusive, much to the opposition's delight. Furthermore they had acquired an orator —a taut, indrawn character, William Pitt—whose speeches, finer than the Commons had heard in generations, burned their way into men's minds. And he had the knack, too, of giving all who listened to him a sense of

[18] Almost the last thing the King did before his death was to give her a large wad of banknotes and certify in his own hand that he had done so.

greatness and glory, made them feel that they were creatures of a destined nation. The Queen's death, the independence of the Prince, the emergence of Pitt, spelt Walpole's doom. Like an old wounded bull he fought bravely, and with a lifetime's cunning: the years dragged on until his inevitable fall came in 1742. On that day in February 1742 when the King prorogued Parliament so that Walpole might resign and power be reshuffled, the first epoch of Georgian England came to an end.

5

The Hanoverian succession was established; not even the early successes of the Jacobite rebellion in 1745 disturbed the confidence of George II or his people. Furthermore the restlessness of the gentry which had done so much to create instability in English governments for many centuries was rapidly disappearing under the influence of the country's growing prosperity—a prosperity which, Pitt thundered, was at stake. Fear of attacks on Hanover emasculated British foreign policy. France grew ever stronger; the world's trade would be gobbled up by her. Her cunning diplomats had baffled Walpole, pretending to peace as they prepared for war. Driven at last to take action against Spain, Walpole had not prosecuted the war with vigour: no success had attended British arms. To many the war was just another war, irritating, expensive, a matter of injured pride and containing little purpose. The merchants knew better; some remembered, and others had learnt of, the riches that came their way during Marlborough's war. They were hot for a declaration against France, eager for the struggle that might lead to the supremacy of the Western world.

These ideas were often incoherent and ill-expressed; they flared up when easy victories seemed to be at hand and were quickly quenched when the trials and disasters of war were heavy on the nation. Only Pitt and a few others had a glimpse of a large future, and that derived mainly from an indefinable sense of grandeur rather than concrete ideas. No one thought in terms of empire in any modern sense, but rather of power and riches and trade. "When Trade is at stake," Pitt had urged, "you must defend it or perish." Yet most politicians could not see events in terms so clearly cut.

The King was Elector of Hanover, and that placed him in a delicate situation both with the Emperor and with Prussia. The King's wishes were never negligible in the eighteenth century, and the King had a natural tenderness for his native land so that, when war came and spread across Europe as it was bound to do, his ministers needed little encouragement to make the protection of Hanover a cardinal principle of military strategy. Pleasing the King was more than ordinary necessity, for Sir Robert Walpole's fall had created a scramble for power amongst ministers and their factions. Pitt found this attitude odious.

Neither justice nor policy, he told the Commons, required us to be engaged in the quarrels of the Continent . . . the confidence of the people is abused by making unnecessary alliances; they are then pillaged to provide the subsidies. It is now apparent that this great, this powerful, this formidable Kingdom is considered only as a province of a despicable electorate.

Pitt's concept of how the war should be fought was quite simple—smash-and-grab raids on the French and Flemish coasts to distract France and so drain troops away from Germany; for the rest, a naval war. He envisaged the destruction of the French fleet, the capture of France's

mercantile marine, and the seizure of her trading bases.
He was only interested in annexation in so far as it brought
strategic bases or rich trade. Naturally the City of London
and the great trading towns were behind him to a man.
Furthermore, Pitt clothed his simple concept of plunder in
language of unsurpassable eloquence; justice, morality,
destiny, all were invoked, and his hearers went away feeling that they were a part of the country's greatness—at
least if they were Pittites.

Others were more sceptical. The King himself was enraged by Pitt and did his best to keep him out of office;
indeed to get any of Pitt's patrons into office required a
ministerial strike on a grand scale. Not that Newcastle
and his brother, Henry Pelham, who had been successful
in wresting a monopoly of power for themselves, were
eager to see Pitt or his friends sharing influence with them.
They regarded Pitt's ideas as rash, expensive, and likely to
plunge the country into everlasting wars. They could not
see how a country so rich and so powerful as France could
be stripped of her trade and possessions. Such a policy,
even if momentarily successful, could only lead to renewed
conflicts. Least of all—and here they were quite wrong—
they did not believe that war led to riches. They had the
conviction, long inculcated by Sir Robert himself, that wars
led to poverty and crippling taxation. Their idea of war
was to limit it as far as possible. The fleet was best engaged protecting the Channel and the Mediterranean for
the sake of commerce; the army's duty was to protect the
King's possessions in Europe. They were not aroused by
projects for attacks on sugar islands, on Quebec, Mauritius,
or Manila, which would eat up ships, men, and money.
The King strongly concurred. He did not like Newcastle
—he always thought him an ass—and he did not like his

brother much better, but they were saints compared with Pitt and his friends, who made their detestable opinions worse by consorting with his loathsome son, the Prince of Wales, who, after a brief period of neutrality on Walpole's fall, was as busy as ever at his old game of making trouble. And when the Prince died, unexpectedly, at Cliveden, through a chill caught playing tennis, his widow went on providing a refuge for opposition politicians; as the King grew older and older her rooms were rarely empty.

The war dragged on. There was never a clear-cut conflict between the two policies—Pitt's and Pelham's; for a time Pitt and his friends were bought off with minor office and a little support given to the "blue-water" policy, as Pitt's ideas were called. Some, indeed, thought that Pitt's furious denunciations were mainly to drive up his own price, and they may not have been entirely wrong, for Pitt was young, needy, and a politician. He was also at times mad, and always emotionally unstable. There were moments when he felt like God, and others when he was so wretched that he could not bear to hear or see a human being. The instability of his temperament made him take refuge in a carefully cultivated theatrical manner which became almost second nature. Add to this the fact that he was highly intelligent, an excellent administrator, but a public idol and monstrously vain: the result was an intolerable colleague and a devastating enemy. He was more of a portent than a politician, but the bewildering years which stretch from Walpole's fall to the King's death in 1760 are peculiarly his.

The ageing of the King made Pitt more formidable, for George II's ministers were naturally more tender towards the opposition, eager to stand well with Leicester House, and incurably hopeful, as politicians are wont to be, of being able to placate the implacable. After the death of Henry Pelham in 1754, all ministers failed to secure a settled system such as Walpole and Pelham had enjoyed. This failure gave Pitt, who was superb at making a nuisance of himself, his opportunity. The reluctance of the old King to receive him was overcome, and for the last three years of George's reign Pitt got his way. His successes for a time suppressed the nattering anxiety of Newcastle; never since Marlborough's day had England enjoyed such victories. Pitt put his trust in bold young men. Wolfe, a dying man, gambled his little army in a last throw. Scrambling up the Heights of Abraham upon which Quebec stood, they surprised Montcalm, smashed his army, and won Canada with its wealthy trade in fish and fur. Rich sugar islands—Martinique and then Guadeloupe—fell to Pitt's squadrons; fell, and handsomely paid their way with increased revenue. Dakar and the French slave trade went the same way. In India, Clive, an even bolder and more tempestuous man than Pitt, won Bengal and trounced the French without any prompting. Even the despised continental army won its victory at Minden: the memory of the defeat at Fontenoy, back in '45, was wiped out at last. Indeed the King's reign closed in a blaze of glory—at least for his people. His own end combined, as ever, farce with tragedy. He fell dead, early one morning, in his water-closet from a stroke brought about by his exertions. In his will he asked that his coffin should be placed by Caroline's; a side was to be removed from each so that their dust might mingle in death—a tender gesture of a man who had loved her deeply in the flesh and never forgotten.

6

And the twenty years of war had worked like yeast in
Britain's economy; coal, iron, steel, shipbuilding and
clothing, all of these industries had risen to new levels of
production; nor had agriculture lagged behind; a plentiful
and good diet, the stimulus of economic opportunity, and a
general improvement in social organisation were beginning
to create favourable opportunities for that rapid rise of the
population which was to be the basis of the industrial
revolution. Few men came to the throne at a moment of
greater exaltation than George III—little wonder that in
his first speech from the Throne he told the assembled
Lords and Commons that he " gloried in the name of
Briton ".

CHAPTER IV

GEORGE III

1760—1820

George III was twenty-two years of age when he succeeded his grandfather but mentally and emotionally he was
little more than a boy. His tutors had found him a difficult
pupil, not exactly unwilling, but lethargic and incapable of
concentration. He was eleven before he could read fluently
and at twenty he wrote like a child. He possessed, however, a strongly emotional nature. He was deeply attached
to his younger brother, Edward, and could not be parted
from him. At eighteen he became infatuated with his
mother's friend and adviser, the Earl of Bute, and insisted on making him Groom of the Stole when he obtained his own establishment in 1756. The relationship
between George III, his mother, and Bute has been the
subject of a great deal of misinterpretation by historians.
The situation, however, has been brilliantly clarified by
Mr Romney Sedgwick in his remarkable edition of George
III's letters to Bute. Like all heirs to the throne George
detested the King's ministers and quickly grew to regard
as traitors those of his mother's advisers who, after winning concessions from George II, had, like Pitt, joined the
administration. Bute was a man of no consequence and
therefore neglected by the Court, and George was able to
resent this neglect more strongly because he charged it
vicariously with his own resentful loneliness. Bute was
exceedingly handsome, well informed, with a taste for
natural history, an adroit, easy man, a glaring paragon of

"THE SECOND STAGE OF CRUELTY"
A London street of 1751, as seen in Hogarth's engraving

GEORGE I   GEORGE II

both from Five Guinea Pieces

GEORGE III
from a Gold Guinea

GEORGE IV
from a Gold Sovereign

GEORGIAN COINAGE

GEORGE I
from a contemporary portrait by an unknown artist

GEORGE II
from the portrait by F. Worlidge

GEORGE II
*from the bust by Louis
Francois Roubiliac,
reproduced by gracious
permission of
H.M. The Queen*

CAROLINE OF
ANSPACH
*from the bust by
J. M. Rysbrack,
reproduced by gracious
permission of
H.M. The Queen*

FREDERICK PRINCE OF WALES AND HIS SISTERS
from the painting by J. F. Nollekens,
reproduced by gracious permission of H.M. The Queen

GEORGE III IN
HIS CORONATION
ROBES
*from the portrait painted
in the studio of
Allan Ramsay*

CHARLOTTE OF
MECKLENBURG-
STRELITZ
*from the portrait by
Peter Edward Stroehling,
reproduced by gracious
permission of
H.M. The Queen*

GEORGE III
*from the portrait by Thomas Gainsborough,
reproduced by gracious permission of H.M. The Queen*

GEORGE IV
detail of the portrait by Sir Thomas Lawrence,
reproduced by gracious permission of H.M. The Queen

CAROLINE OF
BRUNSWICK
*from the portrait
by Samuel Lane*

MRS FITZHERBERT
*from the portrait by
Thomas Gainsborough*

GEORGE IV IN HIGHLAND DRESS
from the portrait by Sir David Wilkie

CAROLINE OF BRUNSWICK   GEORGE IV AS PRINCE OF WALES
from a Wedgwood medallion

GEORGE IV, WHEN PRINCE OF WALES
from the painting by George Stubbs,
reproduced by gracious permission of H.M. The Queen

those virtues which the young Prince felt himself to lack. Indeed, the prince was very conscious of his own shortcomings and he feared the great burden which the old king's death would place on his shoulders. He implored Bute to help him, longed to be corrected by him, and thought that life would be intolerable and the nation ruined if ever Bute were to quit his side. Nor was their friendship ever to be endangered by the Prince's marriage. When the Prince's heart was touched by the fifteen-year-old daughter of the Duke of Richmond, he rushed to Bute for advice.

> I submit my happiness to you, he wrote, who are the best of friends, whose friendship I value if possible above my love for the most charming of her sex; if you can give me no hopes how to be happy I surrender my fortune into your hands, and will keep my thoughts even from the dear object of my love, grieve in silence, and never trouble you more with this unhappy tale; for if I must either lose my friend or my love, I will give up the latter, for I esteme your friendship above every earthly joy. . . . On the whole let me preserve your friendship, and tho' my heart should break, I shall have the happy reflexion in dying that I have not been altogether unworthy of the best of friends tho' unfortunate in other things.[1]

Bute said " no ", George obeyed, and prudence triumphed over the " boiling youth "—prudence and that high sense of duty which was to dominate George's strange, cloudy mind until the dark end of his days. He turned away from his natural inclinations and began to search the Almanach de Gotha for a suitable German Protestant princess.

As in marriage, so in all things, George III wished to be controlled by Bute—the one friend whose advice was always right, who never hesitated to mark his faults or to

[1] R. R. Sedgwick, *Letters of George III to Lord Bute, 1756-66*, 38-9.

remind him of the immense responsibility of his calling. George III was greatly drawn to the solemnity of his position and gravely pondered the burdens which the Almighty had seen fit to place on his shoulders, of whose weakness he was all too conscious. Only if his dear friend stood constantly by his side had he any hope of being able to fulfil his duty. The need for Bute was greater because George III had been brought up to believe that his grandfather was almost a helpless prisoner in the hands of a gang of unscrupulous politicians, who were eager only for the spoils of office and quite indifferent to the nation's wants. He thought this of one of the most successful ministries the eighteenth century was to know, the ministry of Pitt and Newcastle, which seized half the world's trade and laid the foundation of that empire which was to be so great a source of wealth for Victorian England. Nevertheless, George III sincerely believed that Pitt and Newcastle were leading their country to ruin. Pitt was a traitor, "the blackest of hearts", because he had left the opposition gangs which clustered about the Princess of Wales at Leicester House and taken office with Newcastle. The fact that George himself had done well out of this deal—obtaining his own establishment and Bute as his Groom of the Stole—was ignored. Pitt had joined the enemy and was therefore a detestable traitor. Newcastle was little better; to George III the Pelhams were the symbols of that system of faction which heirs-apparent were led by nature to hate. And his father, his mother, and Bute had strengthened his natural repugnance to his grandfather's ministers.

This, then, was the situation when this young man of twenty-two succeeded his grandfather in 1760. He was infatuated with Bute and detested the ministers whom he had inherited. There is no need to look further than this, as so many historians have done who have swallowed the

subtle propaganda of Burke and Horace Walpole and seen
in the changes which took place on George III's accession
a deliberate attempt to subvert the constitution and bring
about a Stuart despotism.

Everyone knew that there would be ministerial changes
the moment the old King died. Indeed Pitt was soon assur-
ing Bute that he asked for nothing but Bute's good offices
in the new reign to " put me in some honourable bystand-
ing office where I have no responsibility."[2] As expected,
the King did everything by Bute, took his advice on every
matter, ignoring other ministers with decades of political
experience. It seemed natural enough that Bute should
fulfil his long-cherished ambition and rise to be First Lord
of the Treasury. Alas, for Bute and George III, the task
proved too great for Bute, even though as a peer Bute
could not take on the offices of Chancellor of the Exchequer and Leader of the House of Commons which
were usually held by the head of the Treasury. The
trouble was manifold. In his own way Bute lacked confidence as his King did. Bute too, like George III, was a
lonely man. For years he had lived on the fringe of the
political world and entirely in opposition. He lacked
powerful friends or strong dependants His group in the
Lords and in the Commons was small and a poor match
for those tough factions which had successfully waged
political warfare since Walpole's day. With the King's
unstinted support he could doubtless have won through
and created a ministerial position as strong as Walpole's
had been, or North's was to be, but he lacked the stomach.
His fears and anxieties and his sense of incompetence
frayed his nerves, undermined his health, and at last com-
pelled him to give up. He hoped to retain his private influence with the King without its public responsibilities.

[2] Sedgwick, op. cit., xvi.

And for a time the King wished this too, and consulted Bute secretly on the problems of personalities and politics which arose. Time, however, was working a change in George; time and marriage.

The first year of George III's reign had been taken up almost entirely by the problem of this marriage. Animal passion and the unique sense of public duty in the need for an heir combined to make the matter one of almost neurotic, compulsive frenzy for George III. In the end he settled rashly and unwisely on Charlotte of Mecklenburg-Strelitz, a dim, formidably ugly girl. George himself regretted her plainness. Like his forebears, a sensual man, he was quickly stirred by feminine beauty but, unlike them, his high sense of morality would not allow him to indulge his fancies. Plain and undesirable as she was George III doggedly fulfilled his marital duties, and they bred child after child. Marriage, however, dutiful as it was, weakened his emotional dependence on Bute who, by 1763, had descended from " dearest " to " dear ". Marriage and time; for George III was a slow developer and his infatuation with Bute was part of a delayed adolescence. By 1763, this intensely emotional situation had been in existence for seven years, a long time for such relationships, the intensity of which is partly the result of their known, if unavowed, transience. By 1766 George III was clear of Bute. He had taken Pitt back into favour and in so doing expressed a willingness to exclude Bute from affairs. Pitt's ministry marks the emergence of a King not yet, perhaps, mature—in some ways he was never to reach maturity—but he had ceased to be open to new experience; his pattern of life had hardened, his habits were formed, his responsibilities known. He had married, produced heirs, experienced ill-health, changed and formed ministries, conducted those day to day affairs,

private and ceremonial, which were to be the burden of
his days. His world was known to him, its terrors diminished with knowledge, and the need for a Bute had
passed.

2

The King's relationship with Bute explains much of the
early years of his reign, but not all, for the policy which
they inaugurated together had vast repercussions. Also
George's youth had other consequences than his love for
Bute. There was no heir, no Leicester House for the dis-
contented and the disobliged politicians to flock to for
plotting and scheming and waiting for their revenge, nor
any prospect at all for many long years. True, the King's
fit of madness in 1765 provoked a flutter of hope and
increased the political stature of his uncle the Duke of
Cumberland, by a few inches, for Cumberland would be
Regent if the King went entirely off his head. His quick
recovery, however, soon extinguished the awakened ambition. Groups out of office, like Pultney and Bolingbroke
before them, had to fall back on other devices. In effect,
there was only one—for the opposition to make such a
confounded nuisance of itself that ministries would feel
the need to buy it off. And the easiest way of becoming a
nuisance was to rouse the public, to bring discredit on the
King and his ministers who, it must be said, provided, as
we shall see, ample material. The success, however, of
these tactics of embarrassment was far, far greater than it
might have been; for various reasons. The principal one
was the incapacity of Bute. A stronger minister would
have quickly made his position in the Lords and the
Commons so impregnable that the public mischiefs of the

Grenvilles and Pelhams and their kind would have remained mere irritants. They unnerved Bute. He began to
imagine for himself the fate of a Buckingham or a Straf-
ford and so played straight into the opposition's hands.
George III himself was as yet too untutored in the political game to be able to strengthen Bute's resolve, as he
afterwards strengthened North's. This weakness of will
at Court was a most powerful fault and led to that
instability at the centre which gave the opposition gangs
their opportunity. Instead of being absolutely determined
to do without Newcastle, Hardwicke, Pitt, Grenville and
the rest, Bute, if not George III, feared that he would fail
or, as he himself admirably phrased it, " tho' in the
bosom of victory, constantly tread on the brink of a
precipice, and this without even the hope of doing
good ".[3]

Sensing this weakness at the heart of politics, the opposition were soon in full cry and the independents and the
cautious place-holders hesitant and watchful; men who
should have been tied to Bute's leadership were allowed
to wander into the neutral side-lines to await the outcome
of the struggle. The fight was bitter because there was
much to fight about. When George III ascended the
throne in 1760, England had recently enjoyed a year of
victories unparalleled in her history, the year of Quebec,
Lagos, Minden, and the rest. The City was jubilant and
the almost certain prospect of the total humiliation of
France was distasteful to few. The years of war had
stimulated England's industrial and agricultural production to new levels. A vision of wealth and glory had been
dangled before the nation. True, a few grumbled; squires
who paid a heavy land tax; clergymen for whom the
Hanovarians were still detestable; convinced Tories who

[3] Sedgwick, op. cit., lxii.

had no relish for Whig victories. Bute and George III
were, however, determined on peace, peace if need be at
any price short of a total return to France of everything
England had won. Although the peace took nearly three
years to accomplish, their intentions were quite clear to
Pitt, who was soon in opposition declaiming with all his
majestic fervour on the folly of such a course. The City
merchants were roused to adulation by the fire, the conviction, the sense of destiny which Pitt's words engendered. They knew, as he knew, that Britain's greatness
was at stake. The merchants of the City were no longer a
small group of extremely wealthy capitalists. Their
numbers had grown; the West Indians, the East Indians,
the bankers, the brewers, were rarely now the same men
under different names as they had been in George I's
day. They now tended to be separate powerful groups of
merchants, as rich as their forbears but more numerous.
And behind the wealthy City fathers were the thickening
strata of the professional classes—attorneys, estate-agents,
doctors and apothecaries and, more importantly, the new
industrialists, the men who were making their fortunes in
steel, cotton, coal-mining, porcelain, and the rest, men
who believed by instinct that England was destined to
great wealth if only her opportunities were not scotched
by the incompetence of her King and his ministers. For
decades the opposition had denounced the graft and wire-
pulling of politics; bitter and virulent pamphlets had ex-
posed abuses in all the institutions of government, usually, it is true, with no desire to reform them, but out of
frustration because the writers were denied their enjoyment. In George I's reign and for most of George II's
these denunciations carried little weight, for most of the
men who felt that they ought to play a part in political
life were involved in it one way or another. By 1760, this

was no longer true. Every year saw an increase in those men of substance who felt that they ought to have a voice in their country's government and yet were excluded from it. A vigorous press, both provincial and metropolitan, had grown up to cater for these men and their attitude to government is underlined by the fact that opposition newspapers had a far greater circulation than those which respectfully deferred to the politics of the ministry. Hence the opposition, and particularly Pitt, had in this growing politically-minded public a new weapon with which to belabour the King's ministers. Its strength was to increase steadily with each year of the King's reign but quite early its force was demonstrated.

The very knowledge that the King intended peace was sufficient to make him unpopular and when he rode to the City to celebrate his marriage his coach was hissed, whereas Pitt's was received with wild cheering. When at last the Preliminaries of the Peace of Paris came to be debated in 1762, Pitt was so sick and ill that he had to be carried to the House and allowed the indulgence of sitting from time to time during his speech, which lasted for three and a half hours. In him the voice of the City spoke. His denunciations were based entirely on commercial strategy.

The ministers seem to have lost sight of the great fundamental principle that France is chiefly if not solely to be dreaded by us in the light of a maritime and commercial power [he told the House], and therefore by restoring to her all the valuable West India islands, and by our concessions in the Newfoundland fishing, we have given her the means of recovering her prodigious losses and becoming once more formidable to us at sea.

Such words were nectar to the City merchants and they

waited for Pitt outside St Stephen's, and cheered him to the echo as he drove home, weary and defeated. Such an acclamation worried both George and Bute; many politicians such as Hardwicke, Newcastle, and Devonshire regarded these manifestations as vulgar and to be deplored. No one, perhaps not even Pitt himself, realised their profound importance. In the same way the sudden eruption of John Wilkes into the political arena failed, too, to make George III or his political advisers realise that the King's inheritance was strangely different from his grandfather's.

3

John Wilkes was a *protégé* of the Earl Temple, the titular head of the Pitt faction. Ugly, witty, vain, he had lived a rake-hellish life on the edge of politics, hoping, as most young men in his situation hoped, that his talents or his nuisance value, or both, would secure him a place and a settled political career. Wilkes, however, lacked both. His father had been a successful merchant, a self-made man, without even remote connections with gentility. That would not, of itself, have been a disadvantage in a man whose nature was both humble and discreet. Wilkes was neither. He loved display; possessed a cutting tongue which he could never curb. Cocking a snook was second nature with him. His bumptiousness rarely took a fall. Utterly self-confident, he refused to be impressed; his quick eye for a weakness immediately found its expression in a savage phrase. Such a nature was bound sooner or later to find itself in sharp conflict with authority. The moment came with the Treaty of Paris; a client of the Temple-Pitt group, he was naturally its bitter antagonist and he denounced it with unparalleled ferocity in his

newspaper, the *North Briton*, and interlaced his denunciation with a few well-directed jibes at George III; in No.
45 he went so far as to hope that the King would not pro-
fane St. Paul's by attending a thanksgiving service there
but stay in his own chapel. Thinking that he had an
excellent case of seditious libel, Halifax, the Secretary of
State, issued a general warrant for the arrest of the authors,
printers, and publishers of the newspaper.

Wilkes responded to this challenge with all the effront-
ery and brilliance of his nature. He was bundled off to
the Tower and from there proceeded not only to claim
that he was wrongfully arrested but also to sue Halifax for
damages done to his property during its search. Naturally
the imagination of the public was caught, and Wilkes
became a popular hero. Eighteenth-century society was
strongly individualistic, and the attack by a single man, of
no particular influence, on the entrenched authority of a
corrupt state went to its head like wine. " Wilkes and
Liberty " became synonymous. Furthermore he created a
focus for discontent, not solely for those prospering
middlemen whose disapproval of English government
grew yearly, but also for the *sans-culottes*, the journeymen
and proletarians who were suffering from the dislocation
of trade caused by demobilisation and disarmament. The
adulation in which Wilkes was held passed into idolatry
when he was triumphant. Mr. Justice Pratt declared general warrants illegal, that reasons of state were not plead-
able in English courts, that a Secretary of State was as
answerable as any other man for his actions. And in the
end Wilkes got his damages and Halifax had to pay. This
triumph has been acclaimed as a victory for liberty, for
English law, for the individual, and Wilkes has become a
part of the mythology of English history. Actually the

truth was seedier. The legal arguments against Wilkes were as strong as those for him; his luck was to be tried by Pratt, a man whose career had been forwarded by that very political gang to which Wilkes himself belonged. Pratt was a client of Pitt, and an enemy of George III and his ministers. Had Wilkes faced Mansfield, as he easily might, then English liberty and English justice and the right of the individual might have suffered a singular defeat.

Naturally George III was infuriated. He had been insulted and the criminal had escaped. George, like most of his family, was a good hater and " that devil Wilkes " came high on his list. He egged his ministers on to bring the devil to book, and to book he was brought. When the agents of Halifax had looked through his papers they had come across an obscene parody of Pope's *Essay on Man*, called *Essay on Woman*. Probably it was not written by Wilkes, who may only have been responsible for some of the footnotes, but he was certainly responsible for its printing. For this he was expelled from the House of Commons and undoubtedly he would have been convicted had he stood his trial. Instead he fled to France. An act of cowardice? In some ways; yet it must be remembered that Wilkes was a very sick man. Attempts had been made on his life and he had nearly been killed in a duel with a professional thug, possibly hired to involve Wilkes in a fight. Popularity was little protection in a world which contained so many bitterly hostile to him. Had he stood his trial, he would have faced Mansfield, and the sentence would have been as harsh as the law could make it. As it was, he was declared an outlaw and everyone, particularly George III, believed that John Wilkes's career had ended. The lessons of this incident did not register on George III's dark and cloudy mind. Indeed he learnt little from the first five years of his reign, save that Bute was not the man to help him govern, that terrible task imposed on him by the Almighty, on whose discharge, whether good or bad, depended the prosperity of his people. If only he could find strong, dependable ministers who thought as he did, all would be well—his unpopularity would disappear; peace and plenty, happiness for all, and a triumphant monarchy would ensue. So it still seemed.

The fury and bitterness of the London mob, the constant insults offered to Bute, his mother, and himself, the hysterical adulation with which first Pitt, then Wilkes, was acclaimed taught George III nothing. He could not bring himself to regard these things as expressions of a deep discontent, they were the results of machinations of evil men intent on vexing him. Nevertheless, the strains on George III himself had been very great indeed; the failure of Bute to protect him in the struggle for power which was waged about him was a grievous blow. To add to the difficulties he fell very ill—the nature of his illness is a mystery as his family kept him closely guarded. The weight of evidence seems to point to his sickness not being of a mental nature, although there were hints to this effect. Nevertheless, in George II's behaviour there are indications—in his anxieties and in his hurried speech —of psychological strain. He found the detail of life so hard to bear, so vastly fretting, so impossible to control without the help of a strong, guiding hand.

Unfortunately George turned from Bute to his uncle Cumberland, in whose entourage was perched the hawk-eyed Pitt, and within a trice the "blackest of hearts" was the "dear friend" with whom George III could not bear to part. George III had chosen as a friend this time a man far, far more unstable than himself. No sooner had he formed a ministry than Pitt, elevated to Chatham, went mad more profoundly and totally than he had ever been. In his few moments of lucidity he pleaded for release from office, "under a health so broken as renders present application of mind totally impossible". George III would not hear of it; for two years he waited patiently for Chatham's recovery and then did his best to prevent him from resigning, in spite of the fact that his ministry was at loggerheads and the government of the country drifting into chaos. George III had decided that his position would be hopeless without Chatham's aid. The fact that he obtained none mattered not at all—the emotional state of dependence was the critical factor. And when at last Chatham went, George III transferred at once to the Duke of Grafton, to whom he was soon writing in those clumsy affectionate terms which he had used to Bute, Cumberland, and Chatham. George III's eagerness to adopt at once any man senior to himself, as a father-image, is a measure of his own lack of confidence in the face of duties for which he had an almost exaggerated respect. The happiness, the destiny of his country rested on the wisdom of his conduct and that of his ministers. So far his reign had witnessed little but trials and disappointments and, George III felt, misunderstandings. Wicked men, like Wilkes, had been responsible for leading the nation astray and undermining its confidence in its King. Had George III known that darker days lay ahead of him it is unlikely that his recovery from his madness would have been so quick or so thorough. Not only did Wilkes return to plague him in a more terrible fashion, but the first outbreaks of violence occurred in America, creating a crisis in government such as England had not witnessed for several generations.

4

Great Britain and America—these words now carry the overtones of nearly two centuries of their separate histories, in which common interests and mutual jealousies and a vast change in the relationship of their greatness have made it almost impossibly difficult to discover the realities of their struggle in the eighteenth century and to do justice to their mutual fears and aspirations, with bias to none. The most important fact to remember is that few, if any, discerned America's future greatness in the seventeen-sixties—not even the Americans. For most Englishmen it was but a sort of remote Puritan Ireland, useful for trade but no more useful than the West Indies, a convenient dumping ground for criminals, whores and bankrupts. Some Englishmen admired the sturdy independence of Americans; it was fashionable to think that the primitive conditions of life there bred a stronger sense of liberty and justice. Like the Corsicans or ancient Spartans they were nearer to nature and therefore were blessed with the heroic virtues. The majority, however, regarded Americans as dependants, as cantankerous, difficult dependants who lacked a proper sense of their own responsibilities. English blood and English money had saved their plantations from being overwhelmed by the French. The pound was hard and the dollar soft, and without English credit the American economy—particularly the vulnerable tobacco trade—would have been in Queer Street. Without the support and protection of England, strategically and financially, many thought the American states could not hope to survive. And yet in spite of the sacrifice of the mother country, America failed to be content to deal only in primary products and ship them in English vessels. Reluctantly, countenance of a sort was given to America's habit of breaking all the navigation laws and pushing their way into trade which Britain considered sacrosanct. And yet these were minor irritants; the plantations were small, and lacked real wealth, power and industry: the French were still there to frighten them. Without England they could never survive. Difficult, rebellious, silly they might be, yet their threats could hardly be taken seriously, for their survival without Britain was inconceivable, so inconceivable that the Americans themselves must realise that it was so. Hence sooner or later a compromise would be found; England needed to be firm in essentials if generous in details. Most of the trouble was due to hot-headed agitators who could be neglected. For the majority of English politicians the first stages of the struggle with America were irritating but not important. Like a chafed skin, with care, it could be ignored for most of the time. For us it is important to realise what the size of the problem seemed to men of the 1760s—and that is difficult to grasp. Certainly it did not loom so large as the problem of the Boers in the late nineteenth century; it bore no comparison with the problem of Ireland in the seventeenth century, though more, perhaps, to Ireland in the mid-nineteenth—like that, a problem which was likely to drag on and on, an irritating complication in English politics, but rarely realised to be so fundamental that it could only be resolved by independence. Indeed there were many politicians who regarded the main importance of the American problem as a way of getting at their own political enemies.

Of course, the Americans, like the Irish, saw things differently, perhaps even more clear-sightedly. After all, they lived with the problem and the English did not.

They were primarily a trading nation, not an agrarian nor an industrial one—and they had built up an excellent coastal, a flourishing West Indian, and a promising European trade. They believed their ships to be second to none, and if unhampered by stupid, antiquated, selfish and prejudiced English regulations would quickly develop into the finest shipping in the world. They had to smuggle, they had to evade, in order to flourish. This they resented. And again they hated their dependence on English currency; the great debts which the tobacco traders had incurred in London were regarded as a subtle English method of bleeding the plantations white. And the British attitude baffled them. It was snobbish and patronising, and kept Americans out of the most lucrative colonial appointments. Sometimes the English enforced their regulations in the most niggling way, and sometimes disregarded the Americans' flagrant breaking of them. Above all there was no comprehension of America's worries, no attempt to understand their difficulties. The British position was based on hypocrisy; under the pretence of protection and tutelage the colonies were being exploited to make rich men in London richer. And, of course, as ever with colonials, there was a sense of inferiority. London fashions, London manners, London wealth created a sense of sophistication, of superior manners and breeding which touched Americans like gall on a wound. And their refuge was to consider the British as corrupt, effete, decadent as well as hypocritical and selfish. Yet none of these things mattered so much as the one great fundamental, that Britain by its constitutional control and economic superiority was the greatest obstacle to a rapid expansion of American wealth. That basic fact made the more superficial irritants intolerable to bear.

The difficulties began immediately after the Peace of

Paris, almost before George III had settled down on his throne. By this treaty Britain obtained, from France, Canada and the great Western plains of the Mississippi and Ohio valleys over which the French had claimed, but not exercised, suzerainty. Yet France was not excluded from North America. Her possession of New Orleans and Louisiana gave her control of the mouth of the Mississippi, and American traders and settlers of the Middle West were bound to live under a constant threat of a French intervention if Britain were again to be involved in war with her greatest commercial rival. And colonists had a knack of not waiting for a formal declaration of war and, when not fighting themselves, they were usually constantly intriguing with Indian tribes, urging them to attack their potential enemies. Such restless conditions were a happy hunting ground for the lawless riff-raff which the more settled colonies ejected. Hence the new territories placed an extra burden on Great Britain; forts would have to be established and maintained. The expense of the Seven Years War had been very great and it was unthinkable to men of the time that the colonies should escape from paying towards expenses incurred by measures to protect them. Unfortunately the taxes which England levied on the colonists had steadily dwindled as the skill of the colonists in evasion grew, so that by 1760 the revenue from the duties of molasses scarcely paid for its collection. In order to improve the situation, the Grenville ministry produced, for almost the first time in British history, a coherent policy intended to settle the whole vast problem; at every point it enraged the colonists.

Professor Alden[4] writes:

During the years 1763-5 the ministry headed by George Grenville goaded the colonists into open

[4] J. R. Alden, *The American Revolution* (1954), 4-5.

revolt by a series of ill-advised measures. It undertook to restrict settlement on and speculation in the
lands beyond the Alleghenies recently won from
France; to maintain a standing army of redcoats of
about six thousand men in America; to compel the
colonists under certain circumstances to provide quarters, supplies and transportation for segments of this
army; to make permanent the offices of two royally
chosen superintendents of Indian affairs who had
largely taken over the management of Indian diplomacy, formerly handled by the colonial governors and
assemblies; to renovate the customs service in America
and to enforce the long laxly executed Acts of Trade;
to expand restrictions upon colonial paper currencies,
so necessary to the colonists if not always properly
regulated by them; to lessen the trade between the
colonies and the foreign islands of the West Indies
by imposing a tax of threepence per gallon upon
molasses imported from those islands; and to secure
a revenue from America through the tax on molasses
and, especially, through the famous Stamp Act.

The Grenville program was not intended to
establish British "tyranny" in America. Parts of it
were not even new, although the stamp tax, long used
in England, was a complete innovation in the colonies.
The motives behind the program were mixed.
Grenville and his associates sought to build more
effective defense against France, Spain, and hostile
Indians; to prevent wars between the colonists and the
Indians; to protect the interests of the British sugar
growers in the West Indies; to assure to the mother
country the benefits of her Acts of Trade; to buttress
and rebuild British authority in the colonies; and to
compel the colonies to assume a larger part of the

financial burdens of the empire. The colonists, however, discerned in the Grenville measures a pattern
of "tyranny". They wished to settle and exploit the
trans-Allegheny West; they detested curbs upon their
commerce; they did not desire to provide quarters,
supplies, and transportation for the redcoats; they
needed a larger circulation of currency; they believed
that they were already contributing their fair share,
directly or indirectly, toward the expenses of empire;
they did not want British authority in the colonies
revived or strengthened. They found a majority of
the Grenville measures to be violations of colonial
charters, well-established customs, and the rights of
Englishmen. In brief, they were "unconstitutional".

The colonists' favourite term of abuse was "tyrannical"
rather than "unconstitutional" and owing to an unfortunate concatenation of events for George III this sense of
"tyranny" was strengthened by the effective protest of
Wilkes against general warrants which occurred at this
time, so that the cry of "Wilkes and Liberty" echoed in
the backwoods of America. Furthermore the propaganda
which Wilkes and his supporters were sedulously cultivat-
ing, that George himself was the leader in a dark con-
spiracy to subvert the constitution and deprive Englishmen
of their ancient liberties, was swallowed wholesale by the
credulous colonists. Nor was the reaction one-sided. The
cries of "tyranny" which went up in America struck
their own responsive chord in the circle of Wilkes's supporters, bringing new justification to their attitude towards
the monarchy. And, in addition, George III had the mis-
chance to become himself the central target of the attacks
of the enemies of his ministers. True, to start with these
were shared with Bute and his mother, but by 1763 Bute
had ceased to be a really effective power in politics. The

rapid change of ministries in the next seven years, and the long period of Chatham's incapacity when the ministry was leaderless, all helped to create the illusion that George III himself was the dominant personality in politics and responsible for the policies of his ministers, who lasted only so long as they did his will—and, of course, the illusion was fostered by opposition propaganda. But its effectiveness can be measured by the way it was readily believed both in London and America. The myth that George III was intent on restoring a Stuart despotism was not the fabrication of later historians but a widespread belief which grew out of the conflict with Wilkes and America.[5]

The effect of this well-judged slander was to bring the personality of the King into the bitter political struggles of his reign in a way that was entirely novel in English life. George I and George II had been lampooned on their choice of mistresses, on their predilections for Germans and for Hanover: at times, principally by Chatham, they had been criticised by implication in the House of Commons, but such attacks were intermittent and fleeting. The bulk of abuse had been borne by their ministers. Wilkes and America, and the ruthless exploitation of these conflicts by an unscrupulous opposition, brought George III himself into the political arena. The opposition was certainly unscrupulous—neither Rockingham nor Chatham nor even Grenville had at any time thought deeply about American affairs and although they stuck to their policies

[5] Cf. *Diary of Sylas Neville*, ed. B. Cozens-Hardy: Neville, a young middle-class man of the same age as George III, had no term of abuse too strong for his monarch or praise too lavish for the Americans—sentiments which were strongly shared by his large circle of acquaintances. Wilkes had compared George III to the Stuarts when talking to Boswell in Naples, 18 Feb., 1765. F. Brady and F. A. Pottle, *Boswell on the Grand Tour, Italy, Corsica, France, 1765-6*, 53.

with monumental obstinacy, they had, except perhaps for Grenville, stumbled on them by chance. And when they captured office they were responsible in their turn for making the intolerable American situation worse. Yet the fabrications of their hack writers and the diatribes of Junius had a substratum of truth, and there was a certain justice in George III's being dragged into the centre of the stage.

As the King matured in the 'sixties, and as he learned to rule, his opinions became more rigid. At the same time he came to regard the burdens of his office as awful obligations imposed on him by a Providence more inclined to justice than to mercy. His was a sacred obligation. The power, the might, the empire of Great Britain, the rights of its Kings, the power of its Parliaments, their joint sovereignty, had to be defended at whatever costs, otherwise he would be unworthy of his ancestors or his children. These principles George III grasped with almost lunatic intensity. Hence any compromise with Wilkes or America seemed to him like a sacrilegious weakness, a betrayal of God's trust. The weaker and more unreliable his ministers appeared to be, the more determined George III became to impose his attitude on them. Time and time again he tried to obtain assurances before consenting to the appointment of prospective ministers, that they were sound on American policy. And George III's American policy was simple—that the colonists must be reduced to absolute obedience, if need be, by the ruthless use of force. Because his own views were so simple and to him so obviously right, George III was enraged and embittered by opposition and regarded men like Wilkes as little better than agents of the Devil. When it is remembered that the King, although stupid and a little mad, was still the fountain of honour, that his approbation was almost essential for a successful career in church or state, that his character was powerful and intense, and that he was single-minded and obstinate, his presence on the throne can only be regarded as a national disaster. A strong minister might have counterbalanced the unfortunate effects of the King's personality and beliefs, and no one would have been more grateful—if we may believe his own words—than George III to have found a man strong enough to bear his burdens and relieve him of their intolerable weight. His tragedy was to have discovered Lord North at a time when both the question of Wilkes and America were flaring up to a new intensity.

Lord North in life and in death has enjoyed an extremely bad press. During his premiership he was subject to the scathing criticism of Junius—perhaps the ablest and most devastating political commentator this country has known—and to the more urbane but no less effective attacks of Edmund Burke. After his death generations of historians followed their lead. In very recent years attempts have been made to rehabilitate North and to view his career with a charitable eye. No amount of apology can, however, explain away the most glaring fact of all—that he was an utter failure, that during the time that he was leader of the House of Commons the fortunes of his country reached the lowest point in modern history. And worse; at no other time did the House of Commons itself come so near to losing the respect of men of goodwill. One can understand, one can pity North. He possessed many admirable virtues; few men had a greater fund of generosity and loyalty. He was a virtuous husband and a devoted father. The ease, the affability of his nature, made him a persuasive speaker; his droll, sly sense of humour won him many friends and took the edge off the animosity of his enemies. Few men within the closed circle of Court and politics enjoyed a greater popularity. Neither did he lack a certain skill in administration and dexterity in finance. As Chancellors of the Exchequer went in the eighteenth century he was a good one. Yet his defects were large and glaring. The fat, rounded body and soft pig-like face were indicative of more than ease, gentleness and affability; they bespoke an indolence that bordered on disease, a physical incapacity for hard work which made his duties so onerous to him that he often begged George III to release him from his burdens. His body, lacking that hard muscular fibre without which no statesman can hope to dominate either men or events, betrayed his temperament. The same lethargy invaded his mind. He was content to accept ideas, opinions, decisions from others, and the strength of character and the sheer obstinacy of George III were as necessary to him as his ease and kindness were to his monarch. At no time had he either the strength or inclination to take a firm and personal control of affairs; rather he searched for excuses for his unhappy lot, and as events became more dire, pleaded to be relieved of his intolerable burden of office.

It has been maintained that he stayed in office only because George III had paid his debts and that, in return, he had promised never to desert his King. This may contain a half-truth, may easily have been the reason why North excused to himself his own vacillation, and his own inability to solve by a decisive act the unhappy dilemma in which he found himself. But there were deeper causes, and the relationship with George fulfilled many unconscious needs of North's character. Throughout his life, as a child, as a youth, as a married man, North had been subject to his father and ruled decisively by him. As with his monarch there had been the same half-hearted protests, the same bewailing which merely seemed to be a call for further subjection. The situation in which he found himself as prime minister answered some of the deepest needs of his nature.

And as Lord North found George III so George III found Lord North; they were as complementary as notes in a chord. As we have seen, George III had searched all his life for a dependable friend, transferring his hopes to new men as the old ones failed—Bute—Chatham—Grafton and then, at last, North, the weakest yet the most dependable of all. On all major questions—Wilkes, America, and the Rockingham faction—North thought as George III did. Their attitudes were instinctively the same, although in details they might be, at times, slightly at variance. They both had a reverent respect for the idea of monarchy; indeed in some ways North's was even greater than George III's. He was prepared to see the King most actively engaged in business and it was the King himself who often had to urge North to play a larger role in his ministry. Once the relationship became intimate and close, it developed qualities which had been absent from George III's earlier devotions. George III had matured during the 'sixties; marriage and fatherhood had helped to dispel some of his sense of insecurity, but more important than these things was the fact that in his slow, deliberate, painstaking way he had learned thoroughly the business of monarchy. He had grasped the nature of politics and found his way through the labyrinth of patronage and cousinhood, growing to understand what could and could not be done, and realising as he went the immense power of the throne. With North beside him he enjoyed the twofold role of monarch and politician, and here, if anywhere, lies the truth of those charges of personal government which have been levelled against him. He wielded no powers that his ancestors might not have wielded; his

regard for constitutional behaviour was as punctilious as
one might expect from a Guelph. These things are true.
Yet his curiosity, his avid interest, his daily, almost hourly
interest, in political activity made him a King with a dif-
ference, made him closer to William III or the Stuarts
than to his own immediate ancestors. This appetite for
politics was sharpened by North's indolent dependence,
and because of North's inability to shield his master, men
in opposition could not help but feel that the Crown was
growing stronger at the expense of the politicians and
that dangerous precedents were being created for the
future. The tragedy of George III lay in his temperament.
His stupidity and obstinacy might have been forgiven, as
these same qualities were in his grandfather, if only they
had been exercised on the trivialities of politics—the pro-
motion of ensigns, the appointment of deans, or the ritual
of the royal lives. But they were not. They were exercised
on fundamental questions of policy and personalities—
fields in which George II had frequently permitted his
own wishes to be overborne without much difficulty. Not
that George III was adamant. His hand could be, and
was, forced, but the warmth of his temperament made it
also seem a far more arduous task to politicians than it had
been in George II's day. Certainly it was a task which
North used all his skill to avoid.

Across the centuries it is difficult to define or assess the
more ephemeral aspects of character. Charm dies with the
possessor, but charm is not the only fleeting characteristic
of personality. Some men create controversy as others
arouse affection. Acts which others can perform without
question, give rise with these men to violent debate. And
so it was with George III. Powers which he had every
right to exercise seemed despotic when employed by him.
It is not remarkable that the grotesque myth that he was

aiming at tyranny should have been so widely believed both so early in his reign and for so long after his death.

It was his misfortune that his nature and his actions could be so misinterpreted as to give substance to the belief; and he was dogged by this further handicap, that North instead of shielding him from the calumnies of his enemies strengthened their case by his supine indolence, by his incapacity to extricate himself from a situation that was as tragic for himself as it was for his country. And finally the policy which North pursued with every encouragement from George III ended in utter disaster. Humiliation after humiliation was inflicted on the nation and its institutions brought into grave disrepute. It is time to turn to the sorry tale of their folly.

6

North inherited his first grave problem—John Wilkes. After his expulsion from the Commons in 1764 and subsequent outlawry, Wilkes had decided to remain in France. He drifted to Italy, found a charming but exacting mistress, and frolicked and fooled away his time with that air of serene cynicism which so amazed and entranced his contemporaries. Wilkes had expected to receive a pardon during his erstwhile champion's—Chatham's—ministry. He was disappointed. Chatham in office developed a reverence for the monarchy, greater even than George III's, and in his lucid moments he had not the slightest intention of irritating his King by suggesting a pardon for Wilkes. Wilkes liked wine, loved women, and was obsessed by talk. He found that both Italy and Paris easily satisfied his needs. True, his tastes were expensive. But it was not the lack of money which brought him back in 1768 although he gave this out as the reason. He needed limelight; he longed for the excitement of controversy; in his nature, as with most extravagantly witty men, there was a crude streak of exhibitionism. He timed his return carefully. The ministry under the Duke of Grafton was extremely reluctant to come to grips with Wilkes. They knew well enough his sting. Wilkes, however, made a conflict unavoidable. He stood at the general election in 1768 as candidate for Middlesex and was overwhelmingly successful. There was no avoiding the struggle. The cumbrous process of the law was set in motion, yet it proceeded with great discretion. The outlawry was quashed on technical grounds, but the old conviction of obscene libel could not be evaded. Wilkes was gaoled for eighteen months, which, for an influential man of wealth, was no great hardship. Indeed Wilkes welcomed his incarceration; it made him a martyr and the ministers tyrants. The electors of Middlesex, fed for years on tales of ministerial corruption and jobbery, and recently inflamed with stories of sinister royal intentions to subvert all liberty, adopted Wilkes as a hero. Time and time again they elected him with overwhelming majorities, as time and time again the House of Commons declared his election illegal. George III was driven almost to hysteria by the gross misrepresentations of his enemies and by the scorn and vituperation of Junius, who made Wilkes's cause his own.

Wilkes's problem was simply solved. Amidst howls of execration, his opponent—Colonel Luttrell—was declared elected by the House of Commons, and that stopped the seemingly endless inflammatory appeals to the hustings. The justice of such a decision was, naturally enough, hotly debated. The friends of liberty saw in it the end of representative government and clamoured for a reform of the House of Commons, which they came to regard as a complaisant tool of the royal will. More sober men saw the force of Parliament's decision. Over the centuries members had fought for its right to decide the composition of the Commons and to control its membership. The fact that Middlesex was a large and democratic constituency was quite irrelevant. They, themselves, must remain judge and, legally, they had a strong case in rejecting a convicted felon. The alternative to declaring Luttrell elected was to disfranchise Middlesex. The formal, legal case for the ministry and for the Commons was overwhelmingly strong, but only obstinate, blind partisans of the government could refuse to recognise that this was also a case for equity. All knew that the prosecutions against Wilkes had been rigged, that he had been hounded and persecuted for trivial misdemeanours. Tories like Boswell and Johnson, authoritarian Whigs such as Hardwicke and Newcastle, could maintain that Wilkes had endangered the constitution and by his dangerous sallies threatened the throne. The man in the street saw him as a victim of prejudiced authority. And although the ministry solved the problem, it was at an enormous cost. They helped to harden the belief that the House of Commons had become the property of a self-perpetuating and corrupt oligarchy in league with a tyrannical king. In the midst of such tribulations Grafton resigned and North, instead of going with him, undertook the burden of office.

Nor had poor North done with Wilkes. A few years later, in the midst of his tribulations with the Americans, Wilkes enticed him into a hornets' nest. It was a question of reporting parliamentary debates. Authority once more was on the side of the ministry. Wilkes was entirely in the wrong. Yet so ineptly did the ministry handle this situation that they deeply affronted the City of London, destroying the records of a court of law; indeed, according to

Chatham, no lover of Wilkes himself, Parliament behaved like a mob. Once more Wilkes had brilliantly twisted George III's tail. " The Devil Wilkes " maddened the King. The latter realised how dangerous was this constant humiliation of himself, of North, and of Parliament, yet his anger clouded his judgement and the supine North, through negligence, allowed himself to be outmanœuvred.

Yet the American story is a sorrier tale. As with human beings who have ceased to love and grown to hate, no compromise was possible; every gesture of reconciliation was vitiated by a withholding of complete surrender which only led to further suspicion and deeper rancour. And when at last riot gave way to war, George III and his ministers had alienated many loyalists and created a unity amongst the colonists, that, frail as it was, would have been impossible at the start of his reign. And he himself had, unfortunately, become the symbol of tyranny, so that the myth of George III's personal despotism has become almost ineradicable in American history. It is improbable that the most skilful statesman could have found a *modus vivendi*, short of complete independence for the colonies, but it was unfortunate for George III himself that his intransigence turned him into a convenient scapegoat.

The story of the war need not be told. The British began by completely underestimating the strength and determination of the colonists. Sandwich dismissed them as " raw, undisciplined, cowardly men ". General Murray thought them " effeminate ". More thoughtful men decided that the Americans lacked the financial and economic resources either to succeed in war or to maintain their independence if they procured it. The ugly prognostications of Wilkes and Charles James Fox that Britain's enemies in Europe would aid America and ruin Britain were dismissed as clamour. George III, North, and the bulk of Parliament, including the country gentlemen, now mostly reconciled to the ministry, were united in their determination to teach the rebels obedience. Disaster followed disaster; France and Spain seized their opportunity to inflict a humiliation on their detested rival. Doubts grew, ministers wondered, then resigned. The opposition, sensing the weakness of North and relishing the prospect of office, exploited the government's difficulties to the utmost. The spectral figure of the sick, half-mad Chatham—"the scarecrow of violence" as he called himself—harangued the Lord on the follies and mismanagements of the war. North, realising that he was caught in circumstances too great for his comprehension, longed to resign, yet his sense of loyalty prevented him from sending more than ambiguous pleas for release which the King rejected. George III could not bear to part with North because that was to recognise his own failure. America would be lost irretrievably and North would be succeeded by a set of men in whom he could place no trust. The situation was more grave, more fraught with danger than many historians will allow. The King held power in his hands. His obstinacy strengthened North; the Court party could dominate the Commons so long as they retained the support of the country gentlemen, whose attitude to America and to libertarian ideals fell little short of the King's. After the passage of Dunning's motion in 1780 in a Committee of the Commons that "the power of the Crown has increased, is increasing, and ought to be diminished", North's fall could only be a matter of time, for into the opposition lobby the country gentlemen had trooped almost to a man.[6]

The need to grant independence and the fall of North

[6] Sir Lewis Namier, *Personalities and Powers*, 76.

as an ardent champion, were many old Tory
mands for annual parliaments, for the ex-
cemen from the Commons and for a stronger
entation.

much of this agitation was organised by men
l politics, its value to the opposition was too
eaders to stay outside its orbit for very long.
ded by the Marquess of Rockingham and his
Edmund Burke, became closely associated
moderate wing of the reforming movement.
attracted by the reform of Parliament itself,
great value to themselves in the radical
he power of the Crown ought to be curbed
s of patronage reduced. They were attracted
: George III was a passionately loyal man
his attachments as in his morality. Even if
in forcing themselves on to the King, his
would render their position insecure. And,
fact that they had exploited the strong
r reform made them doubly odious to the
ess such public agitation helped to bring
d force George III's hand; nevertheless the
very great. George III regarded radicalism
ason, and the name Rockingham became
. In consequence, after the fall of North,
al situation was fraught with danger and
rsonal position became well-nigh untenable.
n for reform had behind it a most solid and
port which at any time might threaten the
e of government if wantonly exploited.
was aware of the power of these extra-
orces, particularly as a weapon to frighten
ompliance with their aims. Nor were the
m merely tools to be used by an opposition

were tragic events for George III, and he sat down to
draft a message of abdication, so conscious was he of his
sense of failure.

> His Majesty during the twenty-one years he has sate
> on the throne of Great Britain, has had no object so
> much at heart as the maintenance of the British Con-
> stitution, of which the difficulties he has at times met
> with from his scrupulous attachment to the rights of
> Parliament are sufficient proofs. His Majesty is con-
> vinced that the sudden change of sentiments of one
> branch of the legislature has totally incapacitated him
> from either conducting the war with effect, or from
> obtaining any peace but on conditions which would
> prove destructive to the commerce as well as essential
> rights of the British nation.[7]

And this was the truth as he saw it. He had a deep regard
for the constitution as it was. He never underestimated his
own rights and duties; at the same time he held Parliament's sovereignty in the highest regard. The rebellion of
the Americans was not only treason to him but treason to
Parliament; treason to the ancient, Providential constitution which both he and his advisers had inherited and
which it was their sacred duty to protect. Once America
had gone, surely, he argued, the rest of the Empire would
follow and even Ireland lag not far behind; and the great
kingdom which he ruled would moulder away, a prey for
the predatory powers of Europe. As Sir Lewis Namier has
so cogently phrased it, "He [George III] is defending
there the vital interests and essential rights of the British
nation."[8] And because he felt that he alone unswervingly

---

[7] *Correspondence of George III*, ed. Sir John Fortescue, v, 425,
no. 3601.

[8] Sir Lewis Namier, *Personalities and Powers*, 41.

followed the path of duty, hampered though he had been by irresponsible, self-seeking men, his failure and its consequences were doubly bitter.

7

Yet truth is relative, and what was so crystal clear to George III was not even discerned by many of his subjects, particularly those who belonged to the more socially and economically aggressive ranks of society. Each decade of Hanoverian rule had witnessed rapid growth in some industry or aspect of commerce, but the new wealth was not easily won. Josiah Wedgwood is typical of his time and class. The son of a potter and yeoman, he possessed sufficient capital to seize the opportunities for his craft in the growing commercial prosperity of the country. By rigorous, almost ruthless, endeavour he overcame formidable difficulties and built up a world-wide trade for his pottery, creating a new and entrancing style bearing the stamp of his own personality. His achievement was based on new methods of technology and a more rational system of production, and also, and perhaps more importantly, by overcoming with the help of like-minded men the formidable problems of transport which all governments had been content to neglect. Now Wedgwood believed that his success was due to scientific experiment, to the steady application of rational principles to all problems, and to riding roughshod over traditional attitudes and ancient prejudices. "All things," he wrote, "yield to experiment."

Throughout the land there were successful men, neither perhaps so overwhelmingly successful nor so vocal as Wedgwood, who felt in the same way. Naturally, how-

ever, the Arkwrights,
that efficiency and the
high dividends. They
of such men as Josep
Darwin, and Benjam
applying reason to th
To these men George
porters were Tories,
moded system of g
dangerous as it was
and Lord North whe
He was not in the
quences of a free A
goods and his worl
rights which preocc
his kind—trivialitie
system of governme
such disastrous cour
begun to read, they h
the corruption of p
tics, for newspapers
ing the opposition'
fellows these vitup
came to believe, and
honest Whig princ
Westminster, nor w
ment were to be re
tailed, and means
Wilkes and the tra
ideas such as these
such a programme
expected, the woul
with many voices,
ideas, such as the

Wedgwood w
concepts—de
clusion of pla
county repres
Although
outside forma
great for its l
The group hea
propagandist,
with the more
They were no
but they saw
theories that t
and the source
for this reason
and as rigid i
they succeeded
hatred of them
of course, the
movements fo
King. Doubt
down North a
price paid was
as akin to tre
hateful to him
the constitutio
George III's pe
The agitatio
respectable sup
whole structu
The oppositio
parliamentary
the King into
forces for refo

as it wished; the disasters of the American war had bitten too deeply into the national consciousness and ministers in office were forced to pay attention to these new influences. The situation was made more dangerous by the nature of the constitution. The King was expected to rule, and George III had every intention of doing so or abdicating. Yet how could he rule with his enemies? How could he survive without them? Above all, how would that system of government over which God had placed him for its preservation be maintained against the ugly threats of irresponsible men? The situation of the King was as tragic as the plight of his country. Both survived. George III and the ancient constitution weathered the storms of agitation and the rage of faction. No one in 1782 could have forecast that this King who was execrated and abused as no King had been since the flight of James II would, before he died, be revered as no monarch had been since Elizabeth I lay dying at Greenwich. This strange turn in the wheel of fortune was largely accomplished by the King himself.

8

George III's tribulations started from the first moment that Rockingham was approached to take North's place. Rockingham stood not only for a reversal of the King's policy—peace with America even at the price of independence—but he was also determined to take legislative action to curb the patronage of the Crown, and this he made a condition of his employment. Loathsome as these conditions were to the King, he was forced to comply. They, of course, increased his hatred of Rockingham's party and strengthened his determination to be rid of them as soon as he could. George III was no dissimulator and Rockingham was quickly aware of the King's difficulties—and his dilemma. If the King had little or nothing to promise, men in minor office were unlikely to support either the King or his choice of ministers without giving due weight to policy. On the other hand Rockingham had his own supporters to consider. Bred as they had been in the pattern of the eighteenth century, they expected their pickings—years in the wilderness had sharpened their appetites. And finally there was the further consideration—not perhaps of exceptional importance—that those sections of public opinion which had supported Rockingham expected a measure of reform.

The result was, as might be expected, a compromise. Burke's Economical Reform Bills (1783) pruned the royal household of some of its more extravagant sinecures; and a great deal was made of excluding customs and excise officers from parliamentary elections. This was done with great flourish and infinite self-congratulation. It gave no pleasure to the radicals and deceived few but nineteenth-century liberals. The measures were largely forcing bids, threats to the King of what he might expect unless he gave his confidence to the Rockinghams and allowed them to settle comfortably in the well-paid royal preserves which they had conveniently overlooked in their purge. The King, however, was brave and obstinate. He showed his mettle by intriguing with the junior ministers in an attempt to get the Burke reforms rejected, suggesting that such matters were best done by regulation and not by Act of Parliament. His attempt was stopped, but it frightened the ministry and made them realise the immense difficulty of governing with a King who was an avowed enemy. Then Rockingham dropped dead—a stroke of luck for the King. To keep out his personal enemy, Shelburne, Charles James

Fox suggested that the cabinet had the right to elect a new prime minister, a suggestion which the King quickly rejected, and Fox resigned: not many of his friends went with him but it created a useful fissure for the King and weakened his enemies. Indeed, they were driven to a desperate and unpopular stroke. In order to bring down Shelburne, Fox allied with North, whom he had spent years castigating. George regarded North's act as utter treachery. Yet he had to accept this "infamous" coalition under the nominal leadership of the Duke of Portland. The coalition's dilemma was worse even than Rockingham's, for the King not merely disliked his ministry, he loathed it. Fox—the real power in the government— intended to check finally the royal power in politics; Portland presented to the King a list of the cabinet and flatly refused to discuss with him appointments to junior offices. The strength of George III's position had consisted almost entirely in his ability to appoint and to discipline his ministerial servants; if that power were to devolve on the cabinet, it was the end of kingship as he knew it. Such a suggestion—in spite of Fox's plea that history was on his side—was novel and revolutionary. It marks a stage in the evolution of constitutional monarchy. Fox saw the impossibility of securing an adequate stability with a ministry which did not enjoy the King's confidence unless George III's right of appointment were to be severely limited, since otherwise a field of intrigue was opened to him which might render any government powerless to continue. George III was as acutely conscious of Fox's intentions as Fox himself. He denied the cabinet's right to appoint junior ministers without consultation. He refused to sign warrants for their appointment.[9] Once

9 For a most illuminating discussion of this crisis and George III's reaction to it, cf. Richard Pares, *King George III and the Politicians*.

more he contemplated abdication and wrote in these terms to the Prince of Wales:

> The situation of the times are such that I must, if I attempt to carry on the business of the nation, give up every political principle on which I have acted, which I should think very unjustifiable, as I have always attempted to act agreeable to my duty; and must form a ministry from among men who know I cannot trust them and therefore will not accept office without making me a kind of slave; this undoubtedly is a cruel dilemma, and leaves me but one step to take without the destruction of my principles and honour; the resigning my Crown, my dear Son to you, quitting this my native country for ever and returning to the dominions of my forefathers.[10]

George III, however, was no longer a rash young man. His heart eased, he settled, or seemed to settle, down to his lot. Utterly indifferent he signed whatever papers the ministry put before him, lulling them into a false sense of security. He regarded himself as a prisoner, forced to do his gaolers' bidding, but quite free to plan escape. And he had a number of cards to play. He was still the fountain of honour, and he flatly refused to ennoble anyone proposed by his ministry. In spite of the attacks of Burke and the insistence of Portland, the King retained his hold on a large number of Court places, which were filled, and would be continued to be filled, by men on whom he could rely. And he was quite prepared to let anyone know that he felt himself to be under duress. His opportunity came in 1783 with the East India Bill; this was highly unpopular and could be interpreted as a further slight by Fox on the Crown. The Commissioners who were to govern India were to be appointed by Parliament, not the Crown, which

[10] Sir Lewis Namier, *Personalities and Powers*, 41.

could not dismiss them. This could be, and was, used to suggest that Fox was attempting to create a personal fund of patronage and that India was to be exploited to keep the Whigs in office. The King struck. Stepping for once outside the limitations placed on him by the conventions of the constitution, he gave an audience to Temple and authorised him to tell any peer that if he voted for Fox's bill in the Lords he would regard him as an enemy. That killed the bill; the Commons exploded with rage; the next day George III sacked his ministry. The fight was on.

George III had shown great political acumen in his timing—the days of the raw, lost youth, utterly dependent on friends for advice, had passed. Years of crises, toil and adversity had turned the King into a master politician as dexterous as he was brave. For many weeks past preparations had been going forward for a general election, preparations of such a thorough nature that the King could be certain of securing a majority for a minister of his choice so long as that minister could demonstrate to the Commons his determination to ride out the storm which his appointment was bound to raise.

The King's choice was William Pitt, son to the Earl of Chatham.

Like his father, William Pitt was keyed to great endeavour by the prospect of battle. Again like his father he had a lofty regard for his own qualities. Yet he was only twenty-four. To choose him as first minister was an act of great bravery, as well as shrewd judgement, for to live through the next months was to require nerves of steel.

Pitt had vast advantages; he had already a reputation for rectitude and for desiring reform. His father had attempted to stand above faction and some of his father's independence and popularity had descended to the son. He was sufficiently clear of commitments to any gang to be welcome to those independents who, much as they had been tired of North, felt that first Rockingham and then Fox were rushing them into anti-monarchical ways which they deplored. Reformers who disliked Fox's personality as well as his methods felt Pitt to be a safer man. He only had to demonstrate his intention to survive to draw to him the support of men whose livelihood depended on the ministry; after them the discreetly ambitious would be sure to follow.

Pitt's own motives in going over to the King after a youth spent in opposition are less easy to discern. His character is difficult to comprehend. He was arrogant, ambitious, and despised the majority of mankind. He loved power for its own sake; wanted it so that he might put into operation those ideas which lay close to his heart. His conviction that he ought to rule was not entirely megalomaniac, for he possessed uncommon capacities. It is often forgotten that his father was a fine administrator. The son was even better. He delighted in the richness of detail and could concentrate his whole attention on the niceties of financial processes. For the desirable if expected prize of ruling his country Pitt was willing to moderate those strong principles to which he had so hastily paid lip service.

Naturally the King and Pitt won the general election of 1784. That was only to be expected, but the King did more than this. Public opinion could express itself in the great populous constituencies and it did so in favour of Pitt and the King. Fox himself only just scraped home at Westminster. Fox never recognised this popular defeat: for him 1784 was a low trick of the monarchy by which it broke his career. Until he died his detestation of George III and of Pitt never abated.

For a time with Pitt it was a honeymoon. He and the

were tragic events for George III, and he sat down to draft a message of abdication, so conscious was he of his sense of failure.

> His Majesty during the twenty-one years he has sate on the throne of Great Britain, has had no object so much at heart as the maintenance of the British Constitution, of which the difficulties he has at times met with from his scrupulous attachment to the rights of Parliament are sufficient proofs. His Majesty is convinced that the sudden change of sentiments of one branch of the legislature has totally incapacitated him from either conducting the war with effect, or from obtaining any peace but on conditions which would prove destructive to the commerce as well as essential rights of the British nation.[7]

And this was the truth as he saw it. He had a deep regard for the constitution as it was. He never underestimated his own rights and duties; at the same time he held Parliament's sovereignty in the highest regard. The rebellion of the Americans was not only treason to him but treason to Parliament; treason to the ancient, Providential constitution which both he and his advisers had inherited and which it was their sacred duty to protect. Once America had gone, surely, he argued, the rest of the Empire would follow and even Ireland lag not far behind; and the great kingdom which he ruled would moulder away, a prey for the predatory powers of Europe. As Sir Lewis Namier has so cogently phrased it, " He [George III] is defending there the vital interests and essential rights of the British nation."[8] And because he felt that he alone unswervingly

---

[7] *Correspondence of George III*, ed. Sir John Fortescue, v, 425, no. 3601.

[8] Sir Lewis Namier, *Personalities and Powers*, 41.

followed the path of duty, hampered though he had been by irresponsible, self-seeking men, his failure and its consequences were doubly bitter.

7

Yet truth is relative, and what was so crystal clear to George III was not even discerned by many of his subjects, particularly those who belonged to the more socially and economically aggressive ranks of society. Each decade of Hanoverian rule had witnessed rapid growth in some industry or aspect of commerce, but the new wealth was not easily won. Josiah Wedgwood is typical of his time and class. The son of a potter and yeoman, he possessed sufficient capital to seize the opportunities for his craft in the growing commercial prosperity of the country. By rigorous, almost ruthless, endeavour he overcame formidable difficulties and built up a world-wide trade for his pottery, creating a new and entrancing style bearing the stamp of his own personality. His achievement was based on new methods of technology and a more rational system of production, and also, and perhaps more importantly, by overcoming with the help of like-minded men the formidable problems of transport which all governments had been content to neglect. Now Wedgwood believed that his success was due to scientific experiment, to the steady application of rational principles to all problems, and to riding roughshod over traditional attitudes and ancient prejudices. "All things," he wrote, "yield to experiment."

Throughout the land there were successful men, neither perhaps so overwhelmingly successful nor so vocal as Wedgwood, who felt in the same way. Naturally, how-

ever, the Arkwrights, Strutts, Boultons, and Watts felt
that efficiency and the application of logical ideas brought
high dividends. They were drawn, therefore, to the ideas
of such men as Joseph Priestley, Richard Price, Erasmus
Darwin, and Benjamin Franklin, men who believed in
applying reason to the problems of politics and society.
To these men George III and Lord North and their supporters were Tories, the diehard champions of an out-
moded system of government, corrupt, prejudiced, as
dangerous as it was absurd. Wedgwood blessed his stars
and Lord North when America achieved its independence.
He was not in the least afraid of the economic consequences of a free America. He believed in himself, his
goods and his world, and the niceties of constitutional
rights which preoccupied George III were to him and
his kind—trivialities. Naturally they disapproved of a
system of government which could lead the nation into
such disastrous courses. Furthermore, since they had first
begun to read, they had learned of the iniquities of faction,
the corruption of patronage and of the cynicism of politics, for newspapers and pamphlets never tired of reiterat-
ing the opposition's diatribes. For Wedgwood and his
fellows these vituperations had the force of truth. They
came to believe, and perhaps they were not far wrong, that
honest Whig principles were no longer to be found at
Westminster, nor would ever be found there, unless Parliament were to be reformed, the power of the Crown curtailed, and means of corruption abolished. The fiasco of
Wilkes and the tragedy of America gave wide currency to
ideas such as these; organisations for the furtherance of
such a programme had come into being, but as might be
expected, the would-be reformers spoke not with one but
with many voices, and intermingled with new and radical
ideas, such as the concept of universal suffrage of which

Wedgwood was an ardent champion, were many old Tory concepts—demands for annual parliaments, for the exclusion of placemen from the Commons and for a stronger county representation.

Although much of this agitation was organised by men outside formal politics, its value to the opposition was too great for its leaders to stay outside its orbit for very long. The group headed by the Marquess of Rockingham and his propagandist, Edmund Burke, became closely associated with the more moderate wing of the reforming movement. They were not attracted by the reform of Parliament itself, but they saw great value to themselves in the radical theories that the power of the Crown ought to be curbed and the sources of patronage reduced. They were attracted for this reason: George III was a passionately loyal man and as rigid in his attachments as in his morality. Even if they succeeded in forcing themselves on to the King, his hatred of them would render their position insecure. And, of course, the fact that they had exploited the strong movements for reform made them doubly odious to the King. Doubtless such public agitation helped to bring down North and force George III's hand; nevertheless the price paid was very great. George III regarded radicalism as akin to treason, and the name Rockingham became hateful to him. In consequence, after the fall of North, the constitutional situation was fraught with danger and George III's personal position became well-nigh untenable.

The agitation for reform had behind it a most solid and respectable support which at any time might threaten the whole structure of government if wantonly exploited. The opposition was aware of the power of these extra-parliamentary forces, particularly as a weapon to frighten the King into compliance with their aims. Nor were the forces for reform merely tools to be used by an opposition as it wished; the disasters of the American war had bitten too deeply into the national consciousness and ministers in office were forced to pay attention to these new influences. The situation was made more dangerous by the nature of the constitution. The King was expected to rule, and George III had every intention of doing so or abdicating. Yet how could he rule with his enemies? How could he survive without them? Above all, how would that system of government over which God had placed him for its preservation be maintained against the ugly threats of irresponsible men? The situation of the King was as tragic as the plight of his country. Both survived. George III and the ancient constitution weathered the storms of agitation and the rage of faction. No one in 1782 could have forecast that this King who was execrated and abused as no King had been since the flight of James II would, before he died, be revered as no monarch had been since Elizabeth I lay dying at Greenwich. This strange turn in the wheel of fortune was largely accomplished by the King himself.

8

George III's tribulations started from the first moment that Rockingham was approached to take North's place. Rockingham stood not only for a reversal of the King's policy—peace with America even at the price of independence—but he was also determined to take legislative action to curb the patronage of the Crown, and this he made a condition of his employment. Loathsome as these conditions were to the King, he was forced to comply. They, of course, increased his hatred of Rockingham's party and strengthened his determination to be rid of them

as soon as he could. George III was no dissimulator and
Rockingham was quickly aware of the King's difficulties—
and his dilemma. If the King had little or nothing to promise, men in minor office were unlikely to support either
the King or his choice of ministers without giving due
weight to policy. On the other hand Rockingham had his
own supporters to consider. Bred as they had been in the
pattern of the eighteenth century, they expected their pickings—years in the wilderness had sharpened their appetites. And finally there was the further consideration—not
perhaps of exceptional importance—that those sections
of public opinion which had supported Rockingham expected a measure of reform.

The result was, as might be expected, a compromise.
Burke's Economical Reform Bills (1783) pruned the royal
household of some of its more extravagant sinecures; and a
great deal was made of excluding customs and excise
officers from parliamentary elections. This was done with
great flourish and infinite self-congratulation. It gave no
pleasure to the radicals and deceived few but nineteenth-
century liberals. The measures were largely forcing bids,
threats to the King of what he might expect unless he gave
his confidence to the Rockinghams and allowed them to
settle comfortably in the well-paid royal preserves which
they had conveniently overlooked in their purge. The
King, however, was brave and obstinate. He showed his
mettle by intriguing with the junior ministers in an attempt
to get the Burke reforms rejected, suggesting that such
matters were best done by regulation and not by Act of
Parliament. His attempt was stopped, but it frightened the
ministry and made them realise the immense difficulty of
governing with a King who was an avowed enemy. Then
Rockingham dropped dead—a stroke of luck for the King.
To keep out his personal enemy, Shelburne, Charles James

Fox suggested that the cabinet had the right to elect a new prime minister, a suggestion which the King quickly rejected, and Fox resigned: not many of his friends went with him but it created a useful fissure for the King and weakened his enemies. Indeed, they were driven to a desperate and unpopular stroke. In order to bring down Shelburne, Fox allied with North, whom he had spent years castigating. George regarded North's act as utter treachery. Yet he had to accept this "infamous" coalition under the nominal leadership of the Duke of Portland. The coalition's dilemma was worse even than Rockingham's, for the King not merely disliked his ministry, he loathed it. Fox—the real power in the government— intended to check finally the royal power in politics; Portland presented to the King a list of the cabinet and flatly refused to discuss with him appointments to junior offices. The strength of George III's position had consisted almost entirely in his ability to appoint and to discipline his ministerial servants; if that power were to devolve on the cabinet, it was the end of kingship as he knew it. Such a suggestion—in spite of Fox's plea that history was on his side—was novel and revolutionary. It marks a stage in the evolution of constitutional monarchy. Fox saw the impossibility of securing an adequate stability with a ministry which did not enjoy the King's confidence unless George III's right of appointment were to be severely limited, since otherwise a field of intrigue was opened to him which might render any government powerless to continue. George III was as acutely conscious of Fox's intentions as Fox himself. He denied the cabinet's right to appoint junior ministers without consultation. He refused to sign warrants for their appointment.[9] Once

[9] For a most illuminating discussion of this crisis and George III's reaction to it, cf. Richard Pares, *King George III and the Politicians*.

more he contemplated abdication and wrote in these terms
to the Prince of Wales:

> The situation of the times are such that I must, if I
> attempt to carry on the business of the nation, give up
> every political principle on which I have acted, which
> I should think very unjustifiable, as I have always
> attempted to act agreeable to my duty; and must
> form a ministry from among men who know I cannot
> trust them and therefore will not accept office with-
> out making me a kind of slave; this undoubtedly is a
> cruel dilemma, and leaves me but one step to take
> without the destruction of my principles and honour;
> the resigning my Crown, my dear Son to you, quitting
> this my native country for ever and returning to the
> dominions of my forefathers.[10]

George III, however, was no longer a rash young man.
His heart eased, he settled, or seemed to settle, down to his
lot. Utterly indifferent he signed whatever papers the
ministry put before him, lulling them into a false sense of
security. He regarded himself as a prisoner, forced to do
his gaolers' bidding, but quite free to plan escape. And he
had a number of cards to play. He was still the fountain
of honour, and he flatly refused to ennoble anyone proposed by his ministry. In spite of the attacks of Burke and
the insistence of Portland, the King retained his hold on a
large number of Court places, which were filled, and
would be continued to be filled, by men on whom he could
rely. And he was quite prepared to let anyone know that
he felt himself to be under duress. His opportunity came
in 1783 with the East India Bill; this was highly unpopular
and could be interpreted as a further slight by Fox on the
Crown. The Commissioners who were to govern India
were to be appointed by Parliament, not the Crown, which

[10] Sir Lewis Namier, *Personalities and Powers*, 41.

could not dismiss them. This could be, and was, used to suggest that Fox was attempting to create a personal fund of patronage and that India was to be exploited to keep the Whigs in office. The King struck. Stepping for once outside the limitations placed on him by the conventions of the constitution, he gave an audience to Temple and authorised him to tell any peer that if he voted for Fox's bill in the Lords he would regard him as an enemy. That killed the bill; the Commons exploded with rage; the next day George III sacked his ministry. The fight was on.

George III had shown great political acumen in his timing—the days of the raw, lost youth, utterly dependent on friends for advice, had passed. Years of crises, toil and adversity had turned the King into a master politician as dexterous as he was brave. For many weeks past preparations had been going forward for a general election, preparations of such a thorough nature that the King could be certain of securing a majority for a minister of his choice so long as that minister could demonstrate to the Commons his determination to ride out the storm which his appointment was bound to raise.

The King's choice was William Pitt, son to the Earl of Chatham.

Like his father, William Pitt was keyed to great endeavour by the prospect of battle. Again like his father he had a lofty regard for his own qualities. Yet he was only twenty-four. To choose him as first minister was an act of great bravery, as well as shrewd judgement, for to live through the next months was to require nerves of steel.

Pitt had vast advantages; he had already a reputation for rectitude and for desiring reform. His father had attempted to stand above faction and some of his father's independence and popularity had descended to the son. He was sufficiently clear of commitments to any gang to be welcome to those independents who, much as they had been tired of North, felt that first Rockingham and then Fox were rushing them into anti-monarchical ways which they deplored. Reformers who disliked Fox's personality as well as his methods felt Pitt to be a safer man. He only had to demonstrate his intention to survive to draw to him the support of men whose livelihood depended on the ministry; after them the discreetly ambitious would be sure to follow.

Pitt's own motives in going over to the King after a youth spent in opposition are less easy to discern. His character is difficult to comprehend. He was arrogant, ambitious, and despised the majority of mankind. He loved power for its own sake; wanted it so that he might put into operation those ideas which lay close to his heart. His conviction that he ought to rule was not entirely megalomaniac, for he possessed uncommon capacities. It is often forgotten that his father was a fine administrator. The son was even better. He delighted in the richness of detail and could concentrate his whole attention on the niceties of financial processes. For the desirable if expected prize of ruling his country Pitt was willing to moderate those strong principles to which he had so hastily paid lip service.

Naturally the King and Pitt won the general election of 1784. That was only to be expected, but the King did more than this. Public opinion could express itself in the great populous constituencies and it did so in favour of Pitt and the King. Fox himself only just scraped home at Westminster. Fox never recognised this popular defeat: for him 1784 was a low trick of the monarchy by which it broke his career. Until he died his detestation of George III and of Pitt never abated.

For a time with Pitt it was a honeymoon. He and the

King were at one on policy—peace, economy, and the
exclusion of the Foxites. Pitt systematically tidied up the
administration; the King was content to allow not only
the Commons but also his own minister to air their views
on reform so long as rejection was certain; bills to reform
Parliament and to abolish slavery provided set pieces for
the display of rhetoric. And with each passing year the
strength of Pitt grew; and then, suddenly, in 1788, the
King's mind broke down. The strains of twenty years of
crises told at last; even the security which he was beginning to feel with Pitt was vitiated by agonising quarrels
with his eldest son, who had made Fox his idol.

9

George III lived a dull domestic life. His sense of duty
kept him hard at work. His pastimes were few—an interest in music, a delight in the technique of agriculture. His
wife was as dull as she was ugly, yet he had remained
loyal, performing his duties as a husband with the same
conscientious application that he applied to kingship, but
with happier results. His brood of fifteen legitimate
children was a record for a British king. He was a devoted
father, so devoted that he could only bring himself with
difficulty to allow his daughters to marry, and they for-
lornly addressed their letters to their brothers from " the
Nunnery ". He regarded them with passionate affection
and called them " all Cordelias ". His sons proved less
easy to govern—like their forbears they possessed
sturdy characters but streaked with instability, verging on
madness. Most of them had a taste for ostentation and a
knack of incurring public odium for their private vices.
From the moment that they entered society their reckless

extravagance, coarse tastes, and brutal habits created sympathy for the ageing King, whose frail mind seemed to be endangered by the wanton behaviour of his dissolute sons. His obvious piety, the dignity which he infused into all royal occasions, his patent honesty, were virtues which the middle class discovered and approved; his obstinacy made him popular at last and his insistence on his royal rights was forgotten.

The tribulations which helped to engender so much public sympathy for the King were not trivial. The King had viewed the development of the young Prince of Wales with great distaste; he had suspected that doctrines, harmful to his own ideas of kingship, were being inculcated by his tutors. He opposed strongly the Prince's demands for a separate household, and when this became no longer possible, managed to keep the Prince on short commons in the hope that he might maintain a rein on his exuberance. None of these actions was carried out with any tact, for tact was not a part of George III's nature. He loved the Prince of Wales as a son and hated him as his heir, so that acts of generosity and moments of compassion were vitiated by an insistence on the Prince's humiliation. As for the Prince, his warm and generous nature could not help responding to the gestures of love. Unfortunately his response to authority was equally violent and unrestrained. This dilemma was nothing new in the history of English monarchy but it was rendered more poignant and absurd by the characters of the King and the Prince.

Unfortunately the Prince emerged into public life in the year of the King's most acute political embarrassment —1783. He was then twenty-one and could no longer be denied the separate establishment for which he had been pleading since he was eighteen. The delay in complying

with his wishes had been fatal. Like other princes before
him he had come to believe that he could get his own way
by embarrassing his father through encouraging the opposition. In Charles James Fox he found more than an ally.
Fox possessed immense charm—the warmth and urbanity
of his character swept men from admiration to love—and
the Prince's effusive nature responded quickly to a temperament that had trapped cooler men. And between the
Prince and Fox were deeper bonds. They were both large,
florid men with a tendency to fat; both were utterly reckless about money; both were drawn to highly emotional,
but physically undemanding, relations with women. In
the broad structure of their nature they could recognise
each other as brothers. To this temperamental attraction
was added the compulsive factor of political need. To
force the King to comply with the Prince's demands discharged the obligations of friendship; it also helped to
hammer home the ministerial subjection of the monarchy.
The King's ministers in 1783 demanded that the Prince
should have £100,000 a year and that the King should
personally discharge his already considerable debts of
£29,000. This came at a time when they had driven the
King from what he regarded as the rightful exercise of
his powers, and his bitterness was doubled. Gossip said
that, on hearing the demands, he had muttered, " I wish I
were 80 or 90 or dead ", and he had written tartly to the
prime minister: " When the Duke of Portland came into
Office I had at least hoped he would have thought himself
obliged to have my interest and that of the Public at heart,
and not have neglected both to gratify the passions of an
ill-advised young man." The King, however, no longer
depended on anger and obstinacy to get his way; he was
far more adroit than Fox or Portland at the game of

politics. The Whigs were apostles of retrenchment, so the King placed them neatly in a cleft stick: he offered personally to give the Prince £50,000 a year, plus the revenues of the Duchy of Cornwall, another £12,000, so long as Parliament paid £50,000 towards his debts. By this means the King avoided both paying the Prince's debts, and having his own civil list drastically reduced; and kept the Prince personally dependent; as advocates of economy the ministry could not refuse to accept his offer. Fox, generous as ever, offered to resign, as he had pledged the Prince £100,000 p.a.: the Prince, not to be outdone, insisted on Fox's remaining where he was. The King won, but did not gain. The Prince took Carlton House, at once embarked on his career of building and rebuilding royal residences that was only to end with his death. Furniture, pictures, silver engaged his attention as well as his horses, clothes, food and wine. One day he would be King and sooner or later the nation would pay. Probably the thought of payment rarely crossed his mind. The richness and beauty of life were irresistible and his thoughtless extravagance grew with its indulgence. The Prince, of course, created a social world. He was open, affable, generous and warm-hearted; extremely elegant, undeniably handsome, an irresistible mimic, he never lacked either sycophants or friends. With Charles James Fox as his unofficial prime minister he became the monarch of the Whigs. In 1784 he welcomed Fox at Carlton House, drawn in triumph in the chariot of liberty after his success in the Westminster election, where he had narrowly defeated the King's candidate. The Prince was to have been the guest of honour at Coke's famous celebration of the Centenary of the Revolution at Holkham in 1788. Wherever the aristocratic cup of liberty was raised the Prince was sure to be. To his extravagance in politics and living, the Prince added his own inimitable extravagance in love.

His impulsive and expansive nature wallowed in the atmosphere of love; once stirred, his heart knew no bounds in its adoration. He was ready to throw himself and his kingdom at the feet of his mistress in return, not so much for surrender, as for love. By the time he met Mrs. Fitzherbert he had been in and out of love, twice, and quickly—youthful encounters as intense as they were brief. Mrs. Fitzherbert was an altogether more serious matter. She was six years older than himself, twice widowed, and reluctant. There was the added difficulty that she was a devout Roman Catholic. Politically and socially it was an appalling entanglement, but the difficulties inherent in its nature merely inflamed the Prince's passion and excited his exhibitionism. In the end he secretly married Mrs. Fitzherbert—an illegal and unconstitutional act, quickly known abroad if hotly denied by his friends, whom he half-deceived. This was in 1785 —a terrible distraction for the King who was just winning through to calmer seas with his youthful prime minister. Nor was this all that the King had to bear. The ostentatious support of Fox and the ridiculous marriage with Mrs. Fitzherbert were lacerating wounds, but salt was rubbed into them by the colossal debts incurred by the Prince— well over two hundred thousand pounds by the time of his marriage. The King, embittered by the Prince's behaviour, refused to help. At last the Prince forced the issue by a typical exhibitionistic display. He closed down Carlton House, hired a cab, and drove off in ostentatious destitution to Brighton with Mrs. Fitzherbert. The King was not impressed but he hinted that if the Prince married, thereby repudiating Mrs. Fitzherbert, money might be forthcoming. This put the Prince on his mettle. He worshipped Mrs. Fitzherbert, ostentatiously but devoutly, and separation was quite unthinkable. In 1787 matters came to a head; the Prince, through his friends, got the question of his debts raised in Parliament. The fact of his marriage was raised in Parliament by a bluff independent. Pitt was alarmed at the possible consequences and for once was relieved by Fox's intervention. The ministry pressed the King to come to his son's aid, and in return for an extra £10,000 from the King, Parliament paid off £100,000 of debts, and, in addition, £60,000 for the building of Carlton House. The Prince had squared matters with the King—but at a cost.

The King's health had always been somewhat uncertain. According to medical opinion he may have suffered from an obscure disease, porphyria. Whatever the cause, the stability of the King's mind had never been very great and the accumulation of strain was beginning to take its toll. The rebellious and intransigent attitude of the Prince and the scandals in which he was so frequently involved were bringing great odium on the royal family. Furthermore the King was ageing, and his ruthless devotion of duty, domestic as well as public, was too great a burden for one whose intellectual and emotional structure was fissured with weaknesses. In October 1788 " the flying gout"—the eighteenth-century doctor's description of his own ignorance—flew from the King's legs to his head and stayed there. He talked faster and faster and rarely slept. The Prince was sent for and the King tried to throttle him. George III's condition deteriorated rapidly and his death was expected. The Prince sat up waiting for it for two nights in succession, fully dressed and resplendent with decorations. The King did not die but they had to put him in a strait-jacket and no one thought that he would rule again.

10

This was the dreamt-of moment. How the hopes of Fox and Mrs. Fitzherbert must have soared! A ministry for one, a throne for the other! Pitt saw his career in ruins; the turmoils of his early political life had taught him that no minister could survive without the compliant regard of the King. Naturally he played for time in the wild hope that George III might recover. He tried to preserve some room to manœuvre by attempting to secure a limitation of the Prince's power, introducing a Regency Bill before the Prince and Fox could secure control of the administration.

Fox denounced this as unconstitutional, insisting that the full prerogatives of the Crown belonged to the Prince by right once the incapacity of the Crown was established. Politicians, remembering the King's previous lunacy, and perhaps even more conscious of what would happen to them were Fox to succeed Pitt, were hesitant about accepting such an uncompromising view of Regency. Pitt had excellent precedents: George I on his visits to Hanover had strictly limited the Regency. Then in the midst of these long drawn-out wrangles the King showed unmistakable signs of recovery. By the end of February he was capable of seeing his ministers and dealing with formal business.

The antics of the Prince and his brothers and their supporters incurred a great deal of odium; their actions seemed despicable to the King and unfilial to the public. And naturally the greater part of the blame fell on Fox and the Prince who was mobbed on his way to the Opera. His coach had only to appear in the streets of London for it to be hissed and pelted.

The sad, mad and injured King became for the first time in his life an object of sympathy and respect. His virtues were suddenly appreciated—his natural dignity, his intensely moral private life, his frugality and the simplicity of his tastes made a strong contrast with the wild extravagances and licentious behaviour of his sons. This new-found popularity was strengthened by the revolutionary movements in France. As soon as the French began to subject their royal family to insult, the British began to discover greater virtues in their own sovereign. Once the two nations were locked in combat the republicanism of the French became an anathema to the bulk of the nation. Both in tribulation and in victory the British looked to the monarchy as to a symbol. The wheel of fortune turned at last in George III's favour: he became the first Hanoverian sovereign to achieve popularity.

Although the behaviour of his sons and the consequences of the French Revolution were largely responsible for his continuing and growing popularity, these were not the sole reasons. His illness made its own contribution. George III never recovered quite completely from his attack in 1788. Furthermore he began to age; and for the years that followed there was about him the tragic aura of a Lear. Betrayed by his children he tottered on the verge of his twilight world, an object of almost universal pity. But the importance of his madness did not lie solely in the fact that it touched the heart. It also stopped the King's detailed interference in politics. The pretence of consultation was kept up; the King at times insisted on his views on appointments, but he no longer possessed the mental stamina necessary for a detailed application to business, and Pitt and his colleagues were able to rule without much consideration for the royal wishes.

This increasing neglect of business by the King meant

that he was no longer so closely associated, even in the opposition's mind, let alone the public's, with policy. And that too increased his popularity. It also led Pitt to a great mistake. From the days of the American war Ireland had caused trouble for British statesmen. During that time a measure of independence had been secured and many feared that the long struggle with France might lead to a further desperate bid by the Irish for full independence, if need be with French help. And these fears were realised when the French landed in Bantry Bay. Pitt's solution of this Irish problem was to apply the methods which had worked so well for Scotland—a parliamentary union combined with a toleration of the religious differences between the two countries, a seemingly sensible solution. The ruling class of Ireland had strong vested interests in the semi-independent government which Ireland enjoyed, and it required considerable bribery as well as tact to get the Irish to agree to Pitt's solution. For the bulk of the population the bait of full toleration for Catholicism was sufficient. The King was aware of the Irish problem, but Pitt did not bother to consult him in detail, so confident had Pitt become of his influence. The King, however, held fast with a maniac's intensity to certain concepts, one of which was the sacred and inviolable nature of his Coronation Oath, and he believed that for him to sign any act which emancipated Catholics from their disabilities would lead to the forfeiture of his Crown. He sent for the Queen and the Princess, read them the Coronation Oath, and told them that the House of Savoy must succeed if he violated it. Naturally Pitt, who was completely committed to emancipation, was forced to resign. The strain of this situation brought on another attack of the King's disease. Although his incapacity was on this occasion short-lived, it gave sufficient warning to the politicians that if they wished to avoid having the Prince and Fox as masters they must exercise the most tender consideration for the King. From 1802 until the King became totally and irremediably mad in 1811 every care was used to shield him from the storms natural to his office—emancipation was never mentioned to him.

The ability of Pitt, the extravagant attitudes of Fox and the Prince, the ageing and mental insecurity of the King, the violent and bloody republicanism of France, these factors had brought about a reversal in the attitude to the Crown. In a system of government in which the King was still expected to rule as well as reign, the changes in personal circumstances were bound to have a powerful effect on the popularity of the monarchy. The years from 1800 to 1820 are a long twilight to the reign of George III. The focus of public attention, as far as the royal family was concerned, was the Prince or his unsavoury brothers. And in this, the story of the first four Georges, there is little more to say of George III, now a pathetic figure in his purple dressing-gown, with his wild white beard and hair, totally blind, totally deaf, playing to himself on his harpsichord and talking, talking, talking of men and women long since dead. As he lost all contact with reality, his bodily health improved and to the Prince, who had waited so impatiently for his throne, he must have seemed almost immortal.

At least George III was free from the intolerable strain of his office, freed too from that crushing sense of duty, and no longer grieved by the sad spectacle of a disreputable heir whom he both hated and loved. It was a pathetic end to a life lived vigorously in what his limited mind considered to be the service of his nation. He was a man of small vision, petty ideas, yet not lacking a certain grandeur even in his madness. During his reign the nation

was humbled as it had not been for centuries, and many
had laid the responsibility for this humiliation at his door.
They were less eager to attribute to his influence the
sudden and startling growth of a new empire or those
victories over France and Napoleon which gave to Britain
in the nineteenth century the supremacy of the world; and
yet few statesmen, certainly not Pitt, were as resolute in
their determination to maintain the struggle against France
as was their King. Even so, the last three decades of
George III's reign can never be so closely associated with
the King himself as the earlier half of his reign. A new
world, based on industrial power, was coming into being,
throwing up a new, powerful, and aggressive body of men
who demanded the leadership of their world as of right.
These men had little use for the trappings of feudal society
and no respect for those institutions of government whose
incompetence was daily illustrated to them. They were
determined to change society and to remould it to their
own desire. Although they looked askance at republicanism, they did not love the monarchy—above all they hated
the Regent, his extravagance, his folly, and the fatuity of
his existence. Few monarchs have started to rule in more
inauspicious circumstances than those in which the Prince
of Wales became Regent at last in 1812.

CHAPTER V

GEORGE IV, REGENT AND KING

1812—1830

An old, mad, despised and dying King,
Princes, the dregs of their dull race, who flow
Through public scorn—mud from a muddy spring—
Rulers who neither see nor feel nor know
But leech-like to their fainting country cling.

SHELLEY

The damnedest millstones about the neck of any Government that can be imagined.—WELLINGTON on George III's sons

A libertine over head and ears in debt and disgrace, a despiser of domestic ties, the companion of demi-reps, a man who has just closed half a century without a single claim on the gratitude of his country or the respect of posterity.—LEIGH HUNT on the Regent

From 1812-1837 the Royal Family was held in almost universal contempt, and public opinion was transmuted into a tradition by the brilliantly malicious sarcasm of Thackeray. No doubt both the Regent and his brothers were ridiculed and caricatured excessively. It is not, however, surprising, for the Prince and his brothers had few merits,[1] and they had added to the old King's tribulations, distracting his feeble mind and arousing his anxiety at a time when he needed ease and calm. It was not that the princes lacked virtues. They were all, except perhaps Cumberland, exceptionally honest, direct, and warm-hearted

---

[1] For George IV's brothers see the sympathetic yet just *The Royal Dukes* by Roger Fulford, and Professor A. Aspinall, *Mrs. Jordan and her Family.*

men. Unfortunately they were incapable of restraint or of subterfuge and, except for Cambridge, as reckless with money as the Regent himself. All of them possessed the singular knack of getting into appalling and disgraceful scrapes. A total lack of inhibition in personal relations was unlikely to make a brood of hot-blooded and extravagant princes very popular.

The Duke of York was a good soldier in a modest way but he frittered away what popularity he had by conniving at the activities of his mistress—a demi-mondaine called Mary Clarke—who dealt in commissions like a broker. The public exposure of this practice was carried out in the glare of a House of Commons enquiry. The Duke of York's army career came to an abrupt end. He spent the rest of his life pursuing the elderly Duchess of Rutland, building palaces which he could not afford and never lived in, and encouraging in George IV an attitude of intransigent Toryism. He was never popular.

Oddly enough, the Duke of Clarence was. He was a patently honest man, indeed, honest to absurdity. He lacked all sense of his position or of propriety. He behaved as he wanted to. When a sailor, he ignored his superiors' orders and startled his father by sailing into Plymouth when he should have been in the West Indies. His language was pointed, frequently obscene, and always worth repeating. He lived at Bushy Park with his actress, Mrs. Jordan, who produced ten FitzClarences with remarkable regularity to swell her brood of illegitimate children. Like all the Princes, Clarence was poverty-stricken and although Mrs. Jordan helped to support herself and children by extensive provincial tours, they were always hopelessly in debt. Neither the poverty, the domestic bliss, nor the frequent births were clothed in decent obscurity. The honesty of Clarence's behaviour was wholly admirable yet the results did not add to the dignity of the royal family. And the honesty itself was carried, perhaps, too far when, realising that his legitimate heirs would inherit the Crown, he ordered Mrs. Jordon out of his house, made a couple of botch shots at English heiresses and then promptly married Princess Adelaide.

The Duke of Kent was a martinet who caused a mutiny in Gibraltar through the severity of his discipline. His love of savage punishments bordered on mania and made him the most thoroughly hated man in the army. His amorous adventures were happier though no more respectable than his brothers. He lived in quiet domestic bliss with a French woman. After twenty-seven years spent in her arms, the Duke of Kent felt the call of destiny, repudiated Madame St. Laurent, married a Princess of Leiningen, and fathered the Princess Victoria. His debts equalled his brothers', but the Prince Regent was always unwilling to help him, so his penury became greater than theirs. The Prince hated Kent for both his hypocrisy and for his intrigues against him. The Duke took the obvious revenge—he outwhigged the Whigs and, vociferously radical, he adopted the socialist views of Robert Owen.

The Dukes of Sussex and Cambridge were innocuous. Sussex was given to ridiculous marriages, Whig principles, and debt, but he was a warm-hearted man—foolish, extravagant, quaint, easy to caricature. There was no evil in him. Cambridge lived mostly in Hanover. Bleak, mean, restrained, and in the end wildly, if harmlessly, eccentric— in a loud bellowing voice he answered promptly any rhetorical question which his Sunday preacher inadvertently inserted into his sermon—nevertheless Cambridge was untypical of his family. He lived within his means and only begat legitimate offspring.

Far more unsavoury was the reputation of the Duke of

Cumberland. Whatever his vices were, they received, unlike his brothers', no ostentatious display. He hid them.
His own family spoke of him with horror. By the time he
died the public was convinced that he had begotten a child
by his sister and murdered his valet. It was wrong on both
counts. The valet, a Roman Catholic goaded to despera-
tion by the Prince's sneers at his religion, hacked at him
with a sabre, not successfully enough to kill him, but with
sufficient violence to expose his brain and render his face
even more sinister. As for his sister, her child was by
Captain Garth, according to Greville "a hideous old
Devil, old enough to be her father and with a great claret
mark on his face". On the Princess Sophia's admission,
Cumberland's behaviour was never more than "imprud-
ent", whatever that may mean. When at last Cumberland
decided to marry he chose a princess so notorious for immorality that Queen Charlotte refused to meet her. As
Cumberland was the most determined of reactionaries, the
radical press enjoyed a field day with the Prince's shortcomings.

Indeed, the royal brothers displayed little sense in the
conduct of their lives; gambling and a wanton, vain-
glorious profusion loaded them all with debts which they
accepted with a cheerful negligence in the hope that they
would be discharged by the nation. All but Cambridge
showed as little judgement or taste in the selection of their
friends as in the choice of their mistresses. Card-sharpers
and crooks, the riff-raff of society, were to be found at their
tables. Few monarchies have struggled under the weight
of such a burden of self-indulgent vulgarity.

In the seventeenth century either at Versailles or St.
James's such behaviour might have flourished without
endangering the monarchy, and the excesses of these Royal
Dukes had been challenged, if not equalled, by the bastards

of Louis XIV. The habits of the French King's children might have been subject to widespread gossip on the fringes of aristocratic society but they never became public property. The extension of literacy, the widespread dissemination of newspapers, and above all the multiplicity of cheap, coloured prints, drawn by some of the ablest and cruellest satirists that have ever lived, gave a publicity that was almost modern to the antics of the royal dukes. Such denigration found a ready market. Britain was for twenty years in the throes of a mighty conflict with France. There were times when defeat seemed near; others when starvation threatened the poor. To the sober middle classes the need for religion seemed greater than ever before; they felt that without its restraining influence the country might not be able to avoid the dreadful experience of France. Irreligion became synonymous with radicalism and with social anarchy. Mr. Wilberforce wrote his *Practical View of the Prevailing Religious System of Professed Christians in the Higher and Middle Classes in this Country contrasted with Real Christianity* which by 1817 had run through twelve large editions. It inculcated a stern morality, and its readers must have shivered with horror as they read of the escapades of the royal family or peered guiltily at some of the obscener caricatures of Rowlandson and Gillray. And those sections of society that were not horrified by the Princes' immorality were made bitter by their wanton extravagance. After the war was over, economic dislocation gave rise to much social misery, not only amongst the very poor, but also amongst the craftsmen and artisans. In the north hunger became a commonplace; outbursts of machinery-wrecking—the only weapon the workers could use to enforce better conditions —were endemic; a harsh radicalism flourished. To men who had to watch their children starve the antics of the

royal buffoons made a mockery of life. In times of such
tribulations, the extravagant publicity to which the royal
family was subjected imperilled the throne. Many men,
even those most sympathetic to the Crown, such as the
Duke of Bedford, thought that in 1820 the days of the
monarchy were numbered. It was George IV's misfortune
that the abuse hurled at his brothers rebounded to his own
discredit. The satirists and critics seizèd on those aspects of
his character and behaviour where the fraternal resem-
blance was strongest, and glossed those few virtues which
maintained a tenuous existence in the decaying hulk of his
once vigorous personality.

2

George IV was not a born politician as his father had been.
His sallies into politics in the early seventeen-eighties were
all couched in personal terms, the result of what he felt to
be his wrongs and the deep-abiding friendship which he
cherished for Charles James Fox. Like his hero, he
revelled too much in the arts of living to acquire the
single-minded devotion to business that the pursuit of
power entails. Furthermore, to have overcome the dis-
advantages of the deliberate exclusion from affairs from
which he suffered would have required a strength of character which he did not possess. Throughout his youth and
manhood he was an outcast from the political world and
by the time he inherited power his interest in politics could
never be long sustained. Had Fox lived until the days of
the Regency, political difficulties as well as social ones
might have been raised by the monarchy. As it was the
King in his constitutional capacity did not unduly trouble
his ministers.

Yet it would be untrue to say that George IV, either as Regent or King, became a mere cipher; he was bred too much in the tradition that it was the duty of kings to rule. In 1812 the Regent, it is true, was only fifty, but his physique was such that he had aged beyond his years. His growing corpulence inhibited a steady application to business; it needed a sense of crisis to awaken his political interest and, as might be expected, it was crises about men rather than events which stimulated him most of all. Because of these periodic eruptions of royal interest, it is necessary to say something of George IV's influence on politics, yet this aspect of his life is so distinct from his major and abiding interests that it needs to be dealt with separately.

3

Naturally the Foxite Whigs, ever mindful of the defeats which they had shared with the Regent in the days of his youth, confidently expected to be called from their long and arid sojourn on the back benches when, in 1812, he assumed what were in fact royal powers. During their long exile from office these Whigs, led by Grey since Fox's death, had lost that suppleness in regard to principle which was the hallmark of a Hanoverian politician of the first rank. They were now rigidly attached to those attitudes which Fox had framed for their consolation: peace with France, the abolition of slavery, the emancipation of Catholics, the reform not only of Parliament but of the countless abuses which littered English institutions. Above all, they held strictly to the doctrine that they must be given *carte blanche* not only about measures but also about appointments—as Fox had once demanded of George III. The year was 1812 and England was about to sweep Napoleon from Spain and Europe. The prospect of victories was sweet to the Regent, as to all princes, and that prospect he did not wish to endanger; and measures upon which the Whigs might insist would certainly have endangered it. Yet the Prince had a long memory and was, after his fashion, loyal. He had to make a gesture to the Whigs even though he had little intention of bringing them into office. He offered them a coalition government which, as he expected, they refused. The war, under the competent guidance of Perceval and Wellington, could proceed to its crowning glory. And for the rest of George IV's reign the Whigs stayed in the wilderness, nursing the seeds of their future greatness. In these weeks of crisis the Regent had shown an adroitness of manner which would have become his father at his most skilful, but such occasions were to be rare. More frequently he resembled his father in his prejudices and his obstinacy. He turned violently against Canning and did his utmost to exclude him from Liverpool's cabinet. When by the concerted efforts of his ministers he was overborne, he wrote that his act "was the greatest personal sacrifice that a sovereign ever made to a subject"—a sacrifice, however, that was identical with those wrung from his forbears.

He hated, of course, Canning's liberal principles as well as his avowed sympathy for, possibly liaison with, the Queen. And, typically, George IV tried working against Canning. As Elector of Hanover, George IV had the right to conduct personally his electoral foreign policy; at Windsor he entertained the ambassadors of France, Russia and the Empire, and allowed his disapproval of his own government's liberal policy to be known—he also complimented Louis XVIII on his vigorous action against the revolutionary movements in Spain. Canning, however, pursued his own foreign policy relentlessly. The King was forced to recognise the new South American republics, and his threats to change his ministry came to nothing. He lacked the courage and resilience of the born politician. He could not endure constant and relentless opposition to his will. Typically he caved in, and like his father before him in the days of his youth began to adore what he had once hated. As soon as George IV had surmounted his antipathy, Canning entranced him; his wit and brilliance were much to the King's taste, and even George IV could scarcely fail to recognise that Canning had raised Britain's prestige in Europe. And with that naïve egoism which is natural to monarchy, George blandly assumed that his greatness had risen with his country's. Wellington had done all that he could to dish Canning's policy by encouraging the King to pursue his more reactionary aims, and so, when Liverpool collapsed in March, 1827, Wellington expected to reap the reward of his secret influence. Much to his chagrin George IV, all enmity forgotten, selected Canning. In dudgeon Wellington resigned his office as Commander-in-Chief. Yet this crisis is a witness to the fact that the personal powers of the monarchy had diminished but little in the past sixty years, no matter how much its public prestige had fallen. The changes which had taken place were largely questions of emphasis, due not so much to the growth of new conventions of the constitution as to the temperament of the King.

This is well illustrated by the dominant political crisis of the last years of George IV's reign. Just as Walpole and Pitt, men of formidable ability and political sagacity, had managed their monarchs magisterially and obtained consent to the policy they desired, so might Canning have done, had he not died suddenly in August 1827. His death bedevilled a difficult situation and illustrates the remarkable influence which personalities could still have in the intimate political world. The question which boiled up immediately after Canning's death was the long deferred question of Catholic emancipation. Repeated failure to secure what the Irish considered to be but a just return for the Act of Union had brought Ireland to the brink of civil war.

On this question, however, the King was adamant. His views were those, he told Peel, of his " revered and sainted father ". The fact that the idea of emancipation had always, when put forward, unhinged his father's mind seems to have sanctified George IV's intransigence, as if in some curious way by this gesture he was to expiate the long years of rebellion towards his father. And although, unlike his father, he could not go off his head when the matter was raised, he could put up a good performance. Fortunately for his kingdom the crisis occurred after he had changed the hapless "Goody" Goderich, who had succeeded Canning, for Wellington; for Wellington's will, at least, provided an adequate defence to royal hysteria. Naturally Wellington's Tory ministers were extremely reluctant to recognise the absolute necessity for emancipation which the outbreaks of riots, following O'Connell's election for County Clare, demonstrated. On this reluctance George IV played with some of the skill of his father. He allowed his own wishes to be widely known and when at last he was forced to allow discussion of this question in the cabinet he hinted broadly at his right to veto, in the hope that such boldness might strengthen the waverers. He was hardened in his obstinacy by the defeat of Robert Peel at Oxford University. Peel had come down in favour of emancipation after a lifetime's opposition and, a man of sincere and deep feeling, he felt that his constituents had the right to pass judgement on his changed attitude. They did so forcibly and he lost his seat in Parliament, much to

the delight of George IV, who disliked the man as much
as his opinions. Emboldened by this event, the King determined to sack his ministry rather than consent to the Bill,
and he sent for his chief ministers. They took the journey
to Windsor with much foreboding and were treated to a
scene which Mr. Roger Fulford has described in words
which cannot be bettered.[2]

He spoke to them for nearly six hours fortifying himself with repeated sips of brandy and water. Threats
to retire to Hanover, tears, and even kisses, were all
tried to shake the ministers' attachment to the Bill,
but all in vain, and the King boldly dismissed them
from office. He was found after the interview by
Lady Conyngham and Kingston[3] lying on a sofa,
utterly exhausted. They pointed out to him that the
opponents of the Bill lacked the strength in the
House of Commons to form a Government and told
him there was no alternative to Wellington. Accordingly, that evening he wrote to Wellington:

4 March 1829

My dear Friend,
    As I find the country would be left without an
administration, I have decided to yield my opinion to
that which is considered by the Cabinet to be for
the immediate interests of the country. Under these
circumstances you have my consent to proceed as you
propose with the measure. God knows what pain it
causes me to write these words.   G. R.

After much whimpering, many protestations, and

[2] Roger Fulford, *George IV*, 2nd ed. (1949), 222: by far the best
life of George IV, written with great verve, elegance, and insight.
[3] For these see below.

obtain more room for his numerous family and for the privacy of its garden, but he had spent next to nothing on its extension or adornment. The restraint of the royal family is quite astonishing if compared with the extravagance of most European monarchs: not only with France and Versailles, but with Prussia—Sans Souci, Austria—Schönbrunn, and even Portugal—Belem.

English kings in the eighteenth century lived in modest, old-fashioned buildings, poorly furnished and containing but few good pictures.[4] To a man with a taste for splendour this situation was deplorable, and George IV decided to repair the omissions of his ancestors. The result was Carlton House, the Pavilion at Brighton, the Royal Lodge at Windsor, the virtual rebuilding of Buckingham Palace, and finally, the restoration on an impressive and grand scale of Windsor Castle. To this must be added the brilliant and beautiful additions to London: Regent's Park, the Nash terraces, the now despoiled Regent Street, and the splendid sweep of Carlton House Terrace, still happily unvandalised. This is a monumental achievement in both senses of the word—the greatest contribution ever made by an English monarch to the enduring beauty of his country. The fact that the motive for much of this work was an ostentatious vanity is irrelevant: vanity is not a rare attribute amongst artists, nor is the desire for ostentation. The pity of it was that the hundreds of thousands which George IV poured into his buildings came at a time of acute social distress. Not that his extravagance increased the burdens of the poor; it did not. In terms of national income the sums which he spent were trivial and if anyone had to bear the weight of his debts it was the tax-paying middle classes. The trouble lay in the contrast between

---

[4] Windsor was an exception, at least for pictures, but the Castle was in a poor condition and the first Georges hardly ever used it.

constant invocations of the Almighty's name, he gave his consent to the Bill on April 10th.

This was but the ghost of his father, for who can imagine George III being so supine or wallowing in public tears? And yet it shows how changeless was both the attitude of the politicians to the monarchy and of the monarchy to the politicians. The King was no cipher—his wishes, almost his whims, were still fraught with serious consequence.

It was fortunate that the physical and mental decay of the King had sapped his willpower. It was more fortunate still that the final crisis about emancipation should have occurred with the Tories in power, for the Whigs were committed to emancipation and that alone prevented an alternative government in the midst of this crisis. Even so the uncompromising attitude of the King had needlessly prolonged a situation of the utmost difficulty and helped to bring Ireland to the verge of civil war. Yet it may be counted an even greater blessing that the King died in the following year. It is idle to speculate on what effects the revered memory of his sainted father might have had on the question of parliamentary reform, but few can doubt that the monarchy would have been placed in jeopardy. With each passing year the mood of the country was becoming more ugly and impatient. The scraps of reform by which the politicians hoped to evade the central issue inflamed rather than assuaged public appetite. Without a redistribution of parliamentary representation there was no hope of securing a redistribution of political and social power. The institution which had served Tudor and Stuart England, with its scattered villages and small towns, had proved itself time and time again to be thoroughly ineffective to meet the needs of an expanding industrial world. And personal monarchy belonged to that archaic world. A hard-working, discreet, and compliant sovereign might have preserved undamaged the eighteenth-century concept of a parliamentary monarchy, but the whims and tantrums of George IV were almost too much for the loyal Duke of Wellington to stomach; they strengthened the determination of the Whigs and radicals that, once power was theirs, the revolutionary concept of Charles James Fox that Kings should reign but not rule, should become as rigid a convention of the constitution as they could make it.

It is difficult to do justice to the political activities of George IV. It is only fair to add that a large section of his subjects believed as he did about all questions of reform, but the example of his father should have taught him that monarchs must not support a dying cause. Perhaps, however, more harm was done by his manner than his principles, by his total lack of dignity or restraint, his shameless mimicry of his servants, the torrent of incoherent arguments, the hysteria, the tears and the prostrations. This grotesque, half-insane exhibitionism revolted all ministries. After the death of George IV, steadily but inexorably the powers of the monarchy were restricted.

4

The obloquy which George IV brought on himself and his office was not primarily due to his political behaviour which, although it alienated his ministers, touched few others. From his youth the King had developed an unhappy genius for getting into situations at once farcical and deplorable. Added to this was a talent for spending money never before equalled in his family, whose long history had been marked by a parsimony which bordered on avarice. The cheese-paring instincts of his father may have bred a revulsion in his son. Whatever the cause, the consequences were alarming. As we have seen, his debts had mounted to nearly £200,000 in a couple of years; this was in addition to the £60,000 a year which he had received from the time that he achieved his separate establishment. Astronomical as these figures seem, a word of caution is necessary. Out of the sixty thousand the Prince had to maintain his court—a large and expensive burden which he could not avoid. Furthermore, his allowance was in essentials no greater than Princes had enjoyed at the beginning of the century, although prices had once more begun to rise. Yet even with this *caveat* his extravagance was considerable, and he never curbed his impulse to gratify his desires, whatever the cost, until he died. Time and time again Parliament had to find great sums— by 1794 he owed £400,000, which had risen to over £600,000 in 1796; in spite of a generous and increased provision by Parliament, including a sinking fund for his debts, they still remained at half a million pounds by 1811. It was only after that highly competent physician Sir William Knighton took charge of the royal finances, as well as the royal health, that any improvement was made in them. It was not only George IV's misfortune to incur debts; he also incurred them spectacularly. His manias were building and adornment, manias not uncommon in Princes—even the temperate and restrained William III had indulged himself a little in sticks and stones, at Kensington Palace and Hampton Court—but it was a mania which had been entirely absent in the British royal family since his day. Queen Caroline had spread herself a little at Kew with her garden and grottos; Richmond, too, had been beautified. George III bought Buckingham House to obtain more room for his numerous family and for the privacy of its garden, but he had spent next to nothing on its extension or adornment. The restraint of the royal family is quite astonishing if compared with the extravagance of most European monarchs: not only with France and Versailles, but with Prussia—Sans Souci, Austria—Schönbrunn, and even Portugal—Belem.

English kings in the eighteenth century lived in modest, old-fashioned buildings, poorly furnished and containing but few good pictures.[4] To a man with a taste for splendour this situation was deplorable, and George IV decided to repair the omissions of his ancestors. The result was Carlton House, the Pavilion at Brighton, the Royal Lodge at Windsor, the virtual rebuilding of Buckingham Palace, and finally, the restoration on an impressive and grand scale of Windsor Castle. To this must be added the brilliant and beautiful additions to London: Regent's Park, the Nash terraces, the now despoiled Regent Street, and the splendid sweep of Carlton House Terrace, still happily unvandalised. This is a monumental achievement in both senses of the word—the greatest contribution ever made by an English monarch to the enduring beauty of his country. The fact that the motive for much of this work was an ostentatious vanity is irrelevant: vanity is not a rare attribute amongst artists, nor is the desire for ostentation. The pity of it was that the hundreds of thousands which George IV poured into his buildings came at a time of acute social distress. Not that his extravagance increased the burdens of the poor; it did not. In terms of national income the sums which he spent were trivial and if anyone had to bear the weight of his debts it was the tax-paying middle classes. The trouble lay in the contrast between

---

[4] Windsor was an exception, at least for pictures, but the Castle was in a poor condition and the first Georges hardly ever used it.

the reckless extravagance and luxurious living of the
Regent and the near-starvation of the labouring poor
which bred in them bitter resentment. The hatred which
the Regent's way of life engendered led to an attempt on
his life in 1817—the first attempt to kill an English
monarch since the Assassination Plot of 1696.

And of course George IV's extravagance was not
limited to building. He furnished his palaces in a style
appropriate to their magnificence. He was an excellent
judge of art, making a superb collection of seventeenth-
century Dutch paintings, and he persuaded his government
when King to purchase for £300,000 the collection of
Angerstein which became the nucleus of the National
Gallery, the portico of which, appropriately enough, came
from Carlton House when it was demolished. His taste in
furniture showed the same admirable judgement. With
the skilful advice of the Marquess of Hertford he bought
up some of the most beautiful examples of eighteenth-century French furniture, so that now the royal collection is
unrivalled. His expenditure on silver was prodigious and
much of it is still in use, although here his taste was less
well-founded and depended more on a personal predilec-
tion which led rather to whimsical ostentation than to
restraint.[5] In his building and collection of pictures and
furniture he was guided by men of excellent judgement:
Henry Holland and Nash were both architects of outstanding talent and the Wallace collection is a tribute to the
splendid taste of the Hertfords. At times, however, and
particularly at Brighton, the whims of George IV had full
rein and the result, for many, is far from pleasing. Some
enjoy the domes and minarets of the Pavilion, its chinois-

---

[5] The English china which he purchased in vast quantities was
wholly admirable. A considerable quantity of it is displayed at
Windsor.

eries and bamboo, the fantastic lotus and dragon chandeliers—an Arabian Nights' fantasy in the decorous proportions of eighteenth-century elegance; but others are
overpowered by the almost vulgar richness of its decoration, the violent blues and deep reds, the gold, the silver
and the glass—a *genre* inappropriate to its setting. When
compared with the domestic achievements of the late eighteenth century, particularly of Adam, the Pavilion creates
an air of uncertainty, the child of bombast and inferiority.
Fortunately its exuberance, one might almost say its vulgarity, is restrained by the admirable sense of proportion
which infused the craftsmanship of Regency England. Yet,
whatever one's judgement may be, it remains a singular
work of art, a more intimate expression of George IV's
temperament than any other of his building projects.[6] It
was a pity that he allowed his furnishers and craftsmen to
charge him almost what they would for their work. The
fabulous chandeliers of the Music Room cost £4290 12*s.*
0*d.* and the same prodigality was lavished on the carpets
and curtains and furniture. Nor was the knowledge carefully concealed from the public; the high cost of the
Pavilion was common knowledge. Nor could the gossip
heighten the luxury of the food that was served there or
the quantities of wine which flowed down the gullets of
its fortunate guests. Carême, one of the greatest of cooks
and a creator of some of the noblest dishes of the *haute
cuisine*, was permitted a free rein regardless of cost. A
dinner party with no special guests might be faced with a
choice from one hundred and sixteen dishes served in nine
courses, together with a multitude of wines. On special
occasions the dinners were more complex and more pro-

---

[6] Opinion on the aesthetic quality of the Pavilion is always likely to
be divided. For an informed and admiring appreciation, cf. Margaret
Barton and Osbert Sitwell, *Brighton*.

longed. Many times these lavish feasts were served when the country was desperately short of food, when agricultural labourers were on the verge of starvation and revolt. The exquisite skill with which the Prince matched his food and wine, the incomparable artistry of Carême, in which a prosperous age might have shared a vicarious pleasure, were as gall and wormwood to an impoverished country fighting desperately in the greatest struggle that it had ever known. Even this exhibitionistic display of self-indulgence might have been forgiven or at least tolerated had the Prince surrounded himself with the intelligence, wit and beauty of the nation. Instead his private life became increasingly a subject for ribald satire, and the men of wit with whom he had spent his youth either died or were dropped. It is true that George IV never lost completely his interest either in literature or verbal repartee (after Charles II he has claims to greater wit than any other English sovereign). He read Jane Austen's novels with pleasure and invited her to view the Royal Library, and he remained addicted to the prose and poetry of Sir Walter Scott until the end of his life. Indeed, no sovereign in modern times has equalled his artistic and intellectual interests; and it is not possible to reiterate too often the fact that he possessed these desirable and amiable qualities. Unfortunately, just as these qualities were swamped during his own lifetime by his flamboyant mode of living and by the pathetic farce of his amorous adventures, so too has posterity ignored them for the more obvious grotesqueries of his existence.

Both restraint and judgement were foreign to George IV's nature. His courtship and capture of Mrs. Fitzherbert with its secret, absurd, and utterly illegal marriage brought out clearly the weakness of his nature. He adored mature women to distraction. When in love, all obstacles had to be swept aside, all considerations of behaviour ignored, so that his love might be fulfilled. The mistress gained, George IV settled into a slightly raffish domesticity. He sought affection rather than sensual delights and the objects of his love became, with the years, older and fatter. His last mistresses—if mistresses they were, and there is considerable doubt in the case of Lady Conyngham —were all grandmothers before he noticed them. With the passing years George IV himself became an immense hulk of a man, heaved into shape by corsets when occasions of state demanded a dignified appearance. In consequence he and his enormous mistresses became a favourite target for the caricaturists who catered as obscenely as they dared for the vulgar taste. And his way of life gave them ample subjects for their skill. The grossness of his body worried him and he avoided as much as he could public appearances. In the privacy of the Royal Lodge or the private apartments of the Pavilion he liked to take his ease in the flamboyant undress which he had designed for himself—magnificent dressing-gowns of riotous colours. In these, lolling on his bed or divan, he received his statesmen as well as his mistresses—and was pilloried for it. It was a misfortune that the needs of his nature and the absence of any self-discipline should have led him to a life that was—pictorially speaking—so ludicrous, and doubly hard that a man so charmed with the surface glitter of existence should have so completely betrayed himself. Once one has penetrated beyond the surface or has shut one's eyes to that which is merely ludicrous, one becomes aware that there is much to respect in George IV's attitude to life. There was in him a capacity to surrender, to offer his heart without thought or care of consequence. And his affections were rarely trivial. After his youth only three, or at the most four, women played any part in his

life, and to all of them he was more loyal and more
devoted than kings were wont to be. And in the affairs of
the heart he, of all men, lacked self-regard; old, fat, pious,
his mistresses might be and to some, objects of mockery,
but for him they were the delight of his life because his
love for them was far greater than his lust. He needed
them as a child needs its mother, to be eased and cosseted
by her skilful affection. And here is the key to his personality. The absence of virility, of manly animal strength,
inhibited the respect of those men—statesmen and soldiers
—to whom the world of power belongs. His lack of mus-
cularity, of physical self-confidence, also made it impossible for him to enter into their world and dominate them
in those ways that their instincts demanded. Yet the sever-
est trials of George IV's life had nothing to do with his
extravagance, nor with his florid ostentation, nor with the
inherent weakness of his temperament. They were due to
the sheer blind chance of his marriage, for which his
father was almost entirely responsible.

5

It is necessary to go back to 1795 to unfold the story of
George IV's marriage, but it so clouded and darkened his
reign and was responsible more than anything else for his
grave unpopularity that I feel that it is best to consider it
by itself and in its entirety. It is true that George IV
married in 1795 in order to get his debts paid off and
increase his income—for that, and the need to obtain a
legitimate heir, an act which his brothers seemed loath to
perform. Few kings have married for reasons more
laudable. Of course, such an act meant breaking his word
with Mrs. Fitzherbert, with whom he had lived as a

married man for more than ten years. His affection for
her had weakened and she can never have expected such a
relationship to last a life-time. As for the theatrical
marriage, she was as aware as anyone that it was devoid of
significance, a gesture, at once silly and romantic, of
George IV's. The withering of affection must always
lead to suffering and the rejection of responsibilities, but
George IV was no more false than most. In his decision
to get married he cannot be accused of behaving dis-
reputably.

The folly of the marriage lay in the choice of his wife
—Caroline, Princess of Brunswick. Having brought himself to the painful decision to marry at all, George IV
plunged forward almost regardless of consequence.
George III was quite content for the marriage to proceed
and Lord Malmesbury, who went over to Germany to
collect the royal bride, sent no word of warning either to
the King or the Prince of the singular Princess he had
found at Brunswick. The Princess was not quite mad,
but wildly eccentric in a way which is not wholly uncommon even in royal families. Like her future husband
she was an exhibitionist, but unlike him her exhibitionism
did not lead to luxury and grandeur. She was coarse-
fibred. She was flamboyant, dirty, and highly sexed. Her
manners were largely of the farmyard and the taproom.
No parents can have experienced quite the same relief as
hers on hearing that she had been selected to be the future
Queen of England—at least if she stayed the course, and
it proved close run.

Malmsbury had been nonplussed to find that the
Princess rarely changed her linen and never washed, and
in consequence stank offensively—and even this blasé old
diplomat was so shocked by her language (times had
changed since the rustic obscenities of Walpole and Queen

Caroline) that he felt it necessary to reprove her. Naturally the Prince was appalled by what he saw. The conscious advocate of good taste and refinement, he was revolted by the Princess's clothes, violent, garish, and cheap, and he found her person noisome. He was overcome on meeting her, turning to Malmesbury, saying, " I am not well, get me a glass of brandy." All the Court remarked on the sharp change in his physical condition brought about by his encounter with the Princess. On 8 April 1795 he went through the marriage ceremony, drugged with drink and looking like a corpse. His bride, on the other hand, relished every moment and behaved with immodest truculence. The wedding was consummated for the first and last time that night, and if in nothing else, proved propitious at least in its timing, for nine months later a daughter —Charlotte—was born to them. After a few months made hideous by mutual recrimination they parted for ever.[7] The Prince was utterly revolted by his wife's presence and his response to life was too immediate and too childish to disguise his repugnance. Nor can he be relieved of all responsibility for the fiasco of his marriage. He had grown enamoured of Lady Jersey, a well-preserved grandmother of forty-two, whose wit, elegance and beauty eclipsed those few charms with which Nature had endowed the Princess. Incapable of restraint, the Prince secured the appointment of Lady Jersey as Lady-in-Waiting to his wife, who made no bones about her knowledge of their liaison.

Of course the breakdown in their marriage was immediately common knowledge and it was easy enough to blackguard the Prince's actions and character. This was the era of his great debts, the time, too, when the fortunes

[7] They both used Carlton House, but only communicated with each other in writing.

of England were desperate, a time of bad harvests and near-starvation. And the Princess, unbalanced as she was, had a flair for public appearance. She loved applause and never resisted the temptation to appear before the public in the guise of a wronged woman. The people of London received her rapturously and the detestation of the Prince grew in volume. Never had the Prince's position been so intolerable or his need for affection greater. Lady Jersey proved too brittle a character to fulfil his needs. He hankered for the security of Mrs. Fitzherbert's charms and pleaded for her to come back to him. After securing papal sanction she returned to his bed. Neither was this moment well chosen—the country was aflame with controversy about Catholic Emancipation. The Princess paraded this new injury by appearing from time to time at the Opera when it was known that the Prince and Mrs. Fitzherbert would be present.

Her life soon gave rise to scandal; rumours of lovers, and soon of children, ran though the gossip-intoxicated drawing-rooms of London, with Mr. Creevey there to note it all down. Matters came to a head in 1805 when Sir John Douglas and his wife told the Duke of Sussex that the Princess had been pregnant to their own personal knowledge. Sussex at once told the Prince, who seized his chance. The King had always liked the Princess. He was offended by neither her manners nor her person. Indeed he had tried to obtain control of the young Princess, his grandchild, so that the Princess of Wales might see more of her; and this had infuriated the Prince. Now the latter took the opportunity to blacken the Princess's character— not an act of which any man might be proud, but there are extenuating circumstances. The aristocratic conventions of the time allowed considerable licence to men as well as women so long as discretion was observed. Even the King is reported to have said that he could have forgiven one attachment and one child.[8] But what shocked him, as it shocked his son, was the general profligacy of the Princess's behaviour. On the Prince's instigation the King set up a committee of the Privy Council to investigate allegations made about her way of life. Although cleared of the charge of having had an illegitimate child, the evidence convinced the King and Queen that she was a thoroughly undesirable daughter-in-law.[9]

Although the King and Queen were convinced, others were not. They saw in the investigation an attempt to disgrace her, a contemptible manœuvre by the Prince of Wales. As the Tories were in office the Whigs became more securely devoted to her cause than most, but even a Tory here and there, such as Spencer Perceval, became the champion of this strange woman. No matter how eccentric her private life became, the public never ceased to adore her. Taking her to their hearts helped to emphasise their hatred of her husband. In 1814 she drifted abroad, much to the Regent's relief. During her life in England after the Delicate Investigation she had behaved with some circumspection. Once abroad her temperament flourished untrammelled. She was forty-six years old—a dangerous age for an unbalanced character. The change of life unhinged the Princess completely. She lived in dotty and vulgar ostentation, lavishing her affection upon a handsome but contemptible Italian adventurer called Pergami.

[8] R. Fulford, *George IV*, 65.

[9] This was termed the *Delicate Investigation*; its chief aim was to determine the paternity of William Austin, a child, as the Princess avowed, and she was not disproved, of one of her menial servants. William Austin grew up under her protection, slept in her bedroom until he was fourteen, went on living in her house until she died and was afterwards incarcerated in a lunatic asylum.

The people of Genoa [Roger Fulford writes] were naturally startled to see a gilt and mother-of-pearl phaeton resembling a sea-shell drawn through their streets by two piebald horses driven by a child dressed like an operatic cherub in flesh-coloured tights. In the phaeton lounged the Princess, a fat woman of fifty, wearing a pink hat with several pink feathers floating in the wind, a pink bodice, cut very low, and a short white skirt which showed two stout legs and a pair of top-boots. The phaeton was preceded by Pergami, dressed to resemble King Murat. . . .

Behind this vulgar parade lay the desire for revenge. The Princess felt herself to be a wronged woman and no one can maintain that she was treated with tact or with common decency once King George III had turned against her. No word was sent to her when her daughter died and she only learnt of the death by chance. And as soon as the young Princess died, the Regent's persecution of his wife—getting foreign princes to forbid her their court, and the employment of spies—intensified. Her behaviour, in those circumstances, was silly in the extreme. She had never possessed a scrap of common sense and her taste was as flamboyant as it was vulgar. Whether or not she slept with Pergami does not matter; the majority of her contemporaries decided that she did, nor did she hesitate to confirm them in their conjecture by wanton and public behaviour. Her royal husband regarded these antics with revulsion. His sense of *amour propre*, dormant where his own antics were involved, responded keenly to the behaviour of others. He wanted divorce and pressed his ministers to get the necessary evidence. Lord Liverpool, an earnest and pious evangelical, was as distressed as the Regent by the Princess's behaviour, but he was loath to stir up the hornet's nest which a divorce was bound to bring. These years, 1817-18-19, witnessed acute distress. Unemployment, rioting, sedition, radicalism and republicanism were rampant everywhere. The Whigs, out of office, could be relied on to make a public martyr out of the Princess, so the ministry proceeded slowly if not delicately. A further inquiry, known as the Milan Commission, was set going. Progress was dilatory even though the evidence was lurid, and the law officers of the Crown were reluctant to undertake a prosecution for fear that the Italian witnesses on whom the case turned would not be reliable under cross-examination. Then suddenly the Regent and his ministry were caught in a crisis. The King, who had been healthily mad, indeed far robuster than he had been when sane, decided to die. He stopped eating and in a few weeks was dead. The Princess was now Queen, and she did not lack advisers to persuade her to claim her rights.

Brougham had been in constant correspondence with her during her self-imposed exile; radical as he was, even he felt nervous about her return and allowed himself to be sent by the ministry to buy her off before she landed. A more vigorous radical, Wood, reached her first; in any case she was shrewd enough to know that if she stayed abroad she was condemning herself. Her arrival in England was received more rapturously than that of any sovereign since Charles II landed at Dover in 1660. She entered London in triumph with the mob cheering itself into riot. The ministry took proceedings and the Queen was accused of adultery and scandalous behaviour. Public excitement was immense. Nothing like it had been seen since the Tudors, and Henry VIII had been quietly efficient with his Queens. This was staged as for Grand Opera. Each day the Queen drove in state to the House of Lords, cheered to the echo. Each day London and the provinces read a verbatim account of the long sordid story of what the chambermaids saw. Brougham, one of the greatest advocates of all time, was at the peak of his form and with devastating skill and irony tore the evidence to shreds. The King, hiding at Windsor, was distracted to the point of nervous prostration, soothed only by the ministrations of his latest grandmother, the pious Lady Conyngham. The caricaturists, who had never lacked material, excelled themselves in good, coarse obscenity—but the target was the King not the Queen. Thousands of men and women hated the monarchy, hated it as a symbol of wanton extravagance in the face of their poverty and degradation. The hardness of the times gave a cutting edge to their hatred which frightened the ministry. The temper of the public and the unreliability of the Italian witnesses brought many peers to a discreet withdrawal from the Lords so that the ministry's majority fell, and went on falling, until on 10 November 1820 it reached nine. Liverpool withdrew the bill and London gave itself up to riot, drink, and bonfires for three days. The mortification of George IV was complete.

He never made a full recovery from this blow. He was ageing fast: his immense corpulence brought on a long series of minor ailments which induced a growing hypochondria. But he made a gallant attempt. The fickle public and the more astute politicians quickly deserted the Queen, and the King stirred a flicker of popularity by staging a fabulous coronation of almost oriental splendour; but it soon died. London hated the King and in his heart he knew that it was hopeless to court popularity there. So he made a bid for his other dominions, and took to royal progresses. At Dublin festivities were cut short by the news of the Queen's death, but the Irish enjoyed the novelty of seeing their King as much as the King enjoyed

displaying himself to them. He paid dearly for his
pleasures, however, for the royal yacht ran into tempestuous weather of singular violence. Nothing daunted, the
King went off to Hanover. He discreetly forgot, however,
that his old friend Beau Brummell was living in debt and
destitution in Calais until he was well clear of the place.
The Hanoverians, not having tasted the whims of royal
behaviour since the death of George II, welcomed George
IV rapturously. He was received theatrically on the
grand scale. Nothing could have been more to his taste.
Next year he paraded Edinburgh in the kilt, resplendent
in the Royal Stuart tartan and flesh-coloured tights, and yet
managed to keep his dignity. The Scots loved it. Quaintly
enough George IV had struck the future note of the
monarchy. Nothing would have persuaded the first three
Georges to set foot in Ireland, Scotland or Wales. The
first two went to Hanover to see old friends, collect new
mistresses, and discharge electoral business. The idea of
courting the public would have shocked them had they
been able to grasp its meaning. But George IV, be-kilted,
be-sporraned, be-tartaned, riding up Princes Street to
Holyroodhouse to the roaring cheers of the loyal Scots, was
showing the way that the monarchy would have to go if it
were to survive into an industrial and democratic society.
No one was more fitted for this role than George IV. He
had an instinctive sense of theatre; the very idea of a
public visit to his dominions was a brilliant intuition. He
loved parades. In private life no man could be more
abandoned, more utterly lacking in self-consciousness or
so oblivious of his dignity. On these public occasions,
however, he responded at once to his audience and became
every inch a King. No man tired less at being on show.
The pity for George was that he was too old. At sixty his
enormous bulk could not stand the pace; his ankles were

not strong enough to support him upright for hours at a
time. It proved dangerous for him to clamber on horse-
back, a damaged knee at Hanover brought on the gout.
And his mind and nervous system were also showing signs
of decay. So the popularity which he clearly sought and
dearly loved escaped him when it was almost within his
grasp. His health made him victim to his old routine; a
quiet domestic life at the Royal Lodge with Lady Conyngham, intermingled with bouts of interference in politics
and a steady absorption in the abiding passion of his life
—building. Windsor Castle was near at hand and he gave
what was left of his mind to its problems. He and Wyatt
between them re-created a noble edifice and the King
furnished the great state rooms and commissioned the
great Lawrence pictures to be painted in a style appropriate to its splendour.

As the dark night of death began to cast its shadows,
the King lost much of his confidence and most of his
ebullience. There were days still when he rollicked with
fun, reducing his friends to helpless laughter with his
mimicry of Robert Peel. But there were those wearisome
days when the King talked and talked like his father,
when he told Wellington that he himself had won Sala-
manca; no one was quite certain whether he was mad or
preoccupied with a long and futile joke. More often he
was morose and subdued, pathetically eager to believe
those consolations of religion which Lady Conyngham
preferred to those of the flesh. Sir William Knighton, his
physician, whose hold over him was nearly absolute, encouraged his piety. In the early months of 1830 the King
began to go rapidly downhill. His heart was fatty; minor
strokes gave way to dropsy. He was tapped, staged a mild
recovery, praised the prayers for his health for their good
taste, was merely irritated and not frightened when

Knighton placed a large Bible by his side to indicate the approaching end. When death came at last, he took it bravely and without regret. So ended a life of consummate self-indulgence, lived recklessly and regardless of convention. He accepted without gratitude the immense privileges of monarchy and shunned its duties. Few Kings have been so hated or so mocked or had their virtues so consistently ignored. For George IV possessed virtues. It was his sincerity which brought him into such scrapes and, what so many forget, regal self-indulgence, particularly in building and in the decorative arts, is almost always to the public advantage. Had both his nature and his time permitted him to graft middle-class virtues on to his sense of theatre he would have become the pattern of modern monarchy. He was born too soon and grew up amidst the most licentious aristocracy that England had known since the Middle Ages. But its end was near; when he died a new world was clamouring to be recognised, in which memories of the Regency and of Georgian England were to be considered scarcely fit for the drawing-room; a world in which his self-indulgent elegance had no more place than the rational and sophisticated age which had given it birth.

A SELECT BIBLIOGRAPHY

This bibliography is not intended for the scholar, who should consult Stanley Pargellis and D. J. Medley, *Bibliography of British History, The Eighteenth Century* (1951), but for the curious general reader. V. H. H. Green, *The Hanoverians* (1948), is an excellent introduction to the period; see also, J. H. Plumb, *England in the Eighteenth Century* (1950). Dorothy Marshall, *Eighteenth Century England* (1962), Asa Briggs, *The Age of Improvement* (1959), and Steven Watson, *The Reign of George III* (1960), are the most satisfactory and up to date general accounts of the period. In spite of its strong Whig bias, and its shortcomings in social and economic history, W. E. H. Lecky's *History of England in the Eighteenth Century* (Cabinet edition 1899-1901) remains the most thorough and the best written history of Hanoverian England.

For economic history there are two splendid books by Professor T. S. Ashton who writes with a grace and clarity rare among economic historians. They are *The Industrial Revolution* (1949) and *An Economic History of England: The Eighteenth Century* (1955). The social life of eighteenth-century England has attracted a host of writers and historians. *Dr. Johnson's England* (1933), ed. by A. S. Turberville, is full of good things. Mrs. Dorothy George, *England in Transition* (1931) and *London Life in the Eighteenth Century* (1925), together with Peter Quennell's *Hogarth's Progress* (1955) and E. N. Williams' *Life in Georgian England* (1962), do much to correct the superficial picture of eighteenth-century England as an age of elegance. For the early nineteenth century there is E. Halévy's fine book, *The History of the English People in 1815* (English ed. 1924). A book which throws great light on eighteenth-century conditions is L. Radzinowics's *A History of English Criminal Law: The Movement for Reform* (1948), as readable as it is scholarly.

Books on Georgian art and architecture are legion; the best to my mind are: John Summerson, *Architecture in Britain, 1530-1830* (1953); Christopher Hussey, *The Picturesque* (1927); *English Country Houses, Early Georgian, 1715-60* (1955); *Mid-Georgian 1760-1800* (1956); and *Late Georgian, 1800-1840* (1958); Sir Albert Richardson, *An Introduction to Georgian Architecture* (1949); James Lees Milne, *The Age of Adam* (1947); Margaret Jourdain, *English Interior Decoration, 1500-1830* (1950) (excellent illustrations); E. K. Waterhouse, *Painting in Britain, 1530-1790* (1953); Sir Kenneth Clark, *The Gothic Revival* (1928); Ronald Paulson, *Hogarth, His Life, Art and Times* (2 vols., 1971).

There is not a good general history of the literature of this period; in some ways Sir Leslie Stephen's *English Literature and Society in the Eighteenth Century* (1904) and George Saintsbury's *The Peace of the Augustans* (1916) remain outstanding, but three books are of greater value: Basil Willey, *The Eighteenth Century Background* (1946); A. R. Humphrey, *The Augustan Age* (1954); and Graham Hough, *The Romantic Poets* (1953). On the other hand there are some excellent lives of literary figures and admirable critical editions of their works and letters among which the most outstanding is the Twickenham edition of Pope.

In a period rich with good biographical studies the first four Georges and their wives have come off rather badly. W. M. Thackeray's *Four Georges* is a brilliant but misleading essay. The two best royal lives are R. Fulford, *George IV* (2nd ed., 1949), and Peter Quennell, *Caroline of England* (1939); Roger Fulford, *The Royal*

Dukes (1933), and Dorothy M. Stuart, *The Daughters of George III* (1939), are also useful for the royal family. John Brooke, *George III* (1972) helps to redress the balance in George III's favour, but is too laudatory. For the question of the King's illness, Ida Macalpine and Richard Hunter, *George III and the Mad Business* (1969). The King's correspondence has been badly edited by Sir John Fortesque, but his letters to Bute brilliantly by Romney Sedgwick (1939). George IV has found an admirable biographer in Christopher Hibbert, *George IV, Prince of Wales* (1972) and *George IV, Regent and King* (1973). George IV's correspondence has been very well edited by Arthur Aspinall, *The Correspondence of George, Prince of Wales* (6 vols., 1963-9) and *The Correspondence of George IV* (3 vols., 1938). The same author's *Mrs. Jordan and her Family* (1951) is valuable. The Hanoverian period is rich in court memoirs. The most outstanding are: John, Lord Hervey, *Some Materials for the Memoirs of the Reign of King George II* (3 vols., 1947), and his *Memoirs of the Reign of George III* (4 vols., 1894). *Diary and Letters of Madame d'Arblay*, ed. A. Dobson (6 vols., 1904-5), is valuable for the Court of George III. There are three collections of correspondence of outstanding importance, the first two in the course of publication by teams of editors at Yale; *Correspondence of Horace Walpole*, ed. by W. S. Lewis (1937-   ): *The Letters and Papers of James Boswell* (1950-   ), ed. by F. A. Pottle and others: *The Correspondence of Edmund Burke* (1958-72), 10 vols. ed. by Thomas Copeland and others.

For politics the publications of the History of Parliament Trust are of immense value, and the introductions to the volumes published so far essential reading for anyone interested in eighteenth century politics. Sir Lewis Namier and John Brooke, *The House of Commons*

1754-90, (1964, 3 vols.) and Romney Sedgwick, *The House of Commons 1715-54* (1970). Sir Lewis Namier, *The Structure of Politics at the Accession of George III* (2 vols. 1929), and R. Pares, *George III and the Politicians* (1953), are of special interest. An indispensable collection of documents, with an admirable commentary, for those interested in political history will be found in E. N. Williams, *The Eighteenth Century Constitution* (1960). Other books on important topics which can be recommended are N. Sykes, *Church and State in the Eighteenth Century*; H. Butterfield, *George III, Lord North and the People* (1950); George Rudé has thrown new light both on John Wilkes and the eighteenth century mobs in two books of great originality, *Wilkes and Liberty: A Social Study of 1763 to 1774* (1962), and *The Crowd in History 1730-1848*. Other books of importance which deal with the politics of the Georgian Age are: John Cannon, *Parliamentary Reform 1640-1883* (1973); J. B. Owen, *The Rise of the Pelhams* (1957); J. Brooke, *The Chatham Administration* (1956); I. Christie, *The End of North's Ministry* (1958); E. C. Black, *The Association* (1963), and Donald Greene, *The Politics of Samuel Johnson* (1960), another original book of far greater importance than its title might suggest. Books, both important and readable, dealing with other aspects of eighteenth century affairs are: A. Wolf, *A History of Science, Technology and Philosophy in the Eighteenth Century* (1938); Robert E. Schofield, *The Lunar Society of Birmingham* (1963); J. R. Alden, *The American Revolution, 1775-1783* (1954); G. M. Jones, *The Charity School Movement in the XVIII Century* (1938); A. Lincoln, *Some Political and Social Ideas of English Dissent, 1763-1800*.

The following biographies provide good as well as instructive reading: James Boswell, *Samuel Johnson* (6 vols. ed. of Birkbeck Hill and L. F. Powell, 1934-50); M.

Brailsford, *A Tale of Two Brothers* (John and Charles Wesley) (1954); G. S. R. Kitson Clark, *Peel and the Conservative Party* (1929); S. Clifford, *The Young Johnson* (1955); R. Coupland, *Wilberforce* (1923); R. W. Ketton-Cremer, *Horace Walpole* (1930), and *Thomas Gray* (1955); Elizabeth Longford, *Wellington: The Years of the Sword* (1969), and *The Pillar of State* (1973); Christopher Hobhouse, *Fox* (1934); Elsie Harrison, *Son to Susannah*; Sir Philip Magnus, *Edmund Burke* (1939); Carola Oman, *Nelson* (1947); J. H. Plumb, *Sir Robert Walpole: The Making of a Statesman* (1956), *The King's Minister* (1961), *Chatham* (2nd. ed. 1965); Louis Kronenberger, *The Extraordinary Mr. Wilkes* (1974); J. Holland Rose, *William Pitt* (2 vols., 1911); John Ehrmann, *The Younger Pitt* (1969); Samuel Smiles, *Lives of the Engineers* (1861-62); Robert Halsband, *Lady Mary Worthy Montagu* (1956); *Lord Hervey* (1973). And finally there is a first-class book on Scotland, T. C. Smout, *History of the Scottish People* (1969).

Although this book list is far from complete and could easily be trebled by the addition of other admirable books on Georgian England, it will serve as a guide for those wishing to read more.

INDEX

Act of Settlement, 46, 47, 50
Act of Union, 145, 157
Adam, Robert, 13, 164
Adelaide, Princess, 150
Aggressiveness, Georgian, 14
Agriculture, 29, 32
Ahlden, Castle of, 41
Alden, Prof., *The American Revolution* (qu.), 113-14
Allworthy, Squire, 25
American War of Independence, 28, 109 et seq., 122
Amusements, popular, 15-16
Angerstein Art Collection, 163
Anne, Queen, 37, 58
Argyll, Duke of, 38, 46, 48, 51
Arkwright, Sir Richard, 129
Arrogance, nineteenth - century English, 35
Art, lack of support for national, 33-6
Aspinall, Prof. A., *Mrs. Jordan and her Family,* 148
Assassination Plot (1696), 163
Atterbury's Jacobite Plot, 65
Augusta, Princess of Wales, 80, 98
Austen, Jane, 32, 165
Austin, William, 171
Austria, 162

Bank of England, 62
Bantry Bay, French landing at, 145
Barton, M., and O. Sitwell, *Brighton,* 164
Baskerville, John, 13
Bath, 32
Bear-baiting, 15

Bedford, Duke of, 153
Bedlam, 16
Belem, Portugal, 162
Bentham, Jeremy, 19, 22
Bernstorff, Andreas Gottlieb, 40
Blackstone, Sir William, 26
" Blue-water " policy, 93
Bolingbroke, Henry St. John, Viscount, 29, 38-9, 46-7, 47, 69, 79-80, 81, 101
Boswell, James, 124
Bothmer, Hans Caspar, Baron von, 39, 40
Boulton, Matthew, 129
Bridewell, 16
Bridgewater, Duke of, 33
Brighton, 141
Pavilion, 162, 163-4
Brindley, James, 13
Brougham, Henry, Lord, 173, 174
Brummell, Beau, 175
Buckingham Palace, 161-2
Bull-baiting, 16, 21
Burke, Edmund, 26, 99, 118, 130, 132, 134
Bushy Park, 149
Bute, Earl of, 96-101, 102, 108, 115
Byng, Admiral John, 14

Cabinet, The, 58
Cadogan, Earl, 46, 48
Calais, 175
Cambridge, Duke of, 149, 150, 151
Canada, 94, 113
Canning, George, 155
Canterbury, Archbishop of, 40

Carême (chef), 164
Carlton House, 140, 141, 142, 162
Caroline of Anspach, Queen, 20, 68, 69, 86-7, 161
 as Princess of Wales, 43-4, 45, 50, 55, 56, 57, 61, 63, 64, 68
 personal character of, 69, 70-1, 72-3
Caroline of Brunswick, Queen, 168-174
Cartwright, John, 22
Catholic Emancipation, 145-6, 154, 157, 170
Charlotte, Queen, 100, 151
Chatham, Earl of: see Pitt, William, the Elder
Chesterfield, Earl of, 17, 50, 76, 82
Chippendale, Thomas, 32, 35
Church, 25
Civil List, 65, 68, 140
Clarence, Duke of, 149
Clarke, Mary, 149
Classical Education, 33-4
Clergy, 25, 102-3
Clive, Robert, 14, 94
Cock-fighting, 16, 21
Coke, Thomas, Earl of Leicester, 140
Commerce, 28, 29, 62, 95, 102-3
Compton, Spencer, 68, 76-7, 82
Constable, John, 34
Constitution, development of the, 58, 133
Conyngham, Lady, 158, 166, 174, 176
Cornwall, Duchy of, 57, 85, 140
Coronation Oath, George III's adherence to the, 145
Court, the, 40, 43, 56, 59, 60, 61, 65, 78, 81

Craftsman, Georgian encouragement for the, 32
Craftsman, The (newspaper), 78, 80
Creevy, Thomas, 170
Cremer, Thomas, 78
Cricket, 16
Crime, 18-19
Cruelty, 16
Cumberland, Duke of, 101, 109, 148, 150-1

Dakar, 94
Darby, Abraham, 21
Darby, Hannah (qu.), 15
Darlington, Charlotte Kielmann-segge, Countess of, 42, 70
Darwin, Erasmus, 129
"Delicate Investigation", the, 171
Deloraine, Lady, 88
Devonshire, Duke of, 85, 105
Devonshire, Georgina, Duchess of, 16
Disease, 17
Dorset, Duchess of, 68
Douglas, Sir John, 170
Dublin, 174

East India Bill (1783), 134
East India Company, 27
Economical Reform Bills (1783), 132
Edinburgh, 175
Education, 33-4
Egremont, Earl of, 32
Excise Crisis (1733), 84

"Fifteen", the, 46
FitzClarence family, 149
Fitzherbert, Mrs., 141-2, 165-6, 167-8, 170
Fontenoy, Battle of, 94
Fox, Charles James, 16, 125,

132-3, 136, 139, 142, 143, 146,
153, 154, 160
France, 14, 29, 38, 83, 90, 91-2,
94, 102, 104, 113, 126, 154
Franklin, Benjamin, 129
French land at Bantry Bay, 145
French Revolution, 144
Fulford, R., *George IV* (qu.),
158, 171, 172
The Royal Dukes, 148
Furniture, 32, 33

Gainsborough, Thomas, 14
Gambling, 16, 42
Garth, Captain, 151
Gentry, 25, 81
George I, 19, 23, 25. Chap. II
George II, 19, Chap. III
  as Prince of Wales, 43-4, 50-1,
  55-7, 61-2
  personal character, 69-72
George III, 18, 19, 25. Chap.
  IV
  American policy, 113-18
  death of, 173
  family, 137-8
  madness of, 105, 142, 143,
  144
  marriage, effect of, 100
  personal character, 96-101,
  137
George IV, 18. Chap. V
  as Prince of Wales, 138 et
  seq.
  as Regent, 147 et seq.
  architectural achievements, 162
  et seq.
  attempted assassination of,
  163
  debts, 139-40, 161
  extravagance, 160-1, 162-3
  in Highland dress, 179
  marriage, 167 et seq.
  mistresses, 165-6, 167, 169-
  70

taste in art, 163
Gibbon, Edward, 35
Gibbons, Grinling, 33
Gibraltar, 150
Gillray, James, 14, 152
Gloucestershire   Riots   (1734),
  15
Goderich, Viscount, 157
" Goose-riding ", 16
Government, 18, 20, 24
Grafton, Duke of, 109
" Grand Tour ", the, 34
Gray, Thomas (qu.), 24
Grenville, George, 102, 113,
  114, 116, 117
Greville, Charles C. Fulke, 151
Grey, Earl, 154
Guadeloupe, 94
Guy, Thomas, 63

Habeas Corpus Act, 56
Halifax, Earl of, Charles Mon-
  tagu, 45
Halifax, Earl of, George Dunk,
  106
Hampton Court, 161
Handel, George Frederick, 72
Hanging, 16
Hanover, 30, 39, 50, 51, 62, 91,
  143, 150, 175
  English hostility to, 83
Hardwicke, Earl of, 88, 102,
  105, 124
Harley, Robert, Earl of Oxford,
  29, 37, 54
Harrogate, 32
Hepburn, Dr. George, 78
Hertford, Marquess of, 163
Hervey, Lord, 71, 76
  Memoirs of, 86
Hogarth, 14
Holkham Hall, 140
Holland, Henry, Lord, 22, 163
Horse-racing, 16
Houghton, Norfolk, 77

House of Commons, 74, 123
    demand for reform of, 124
Howard, John, 22
Howard, Henrietta, Countess of
    Suffolk, 70, 82

India, 94
Industrial Revolution, 30-1
Industrialists, the new, 103
Ireland, 46, 88, 145, 157
Isolation, England's cultural, 35

Jacobite Rebellion, 46, 50, 90
Jacobitism, 53, 65, 90
James II, 48
James III, 37, 47
Jenyns, Soame, 26
Jersey, Lady, 169
Johnson, Dr. Samuel, 25, 124
Jordan, Mrs., 149
Junius, 118, 123

Kauffman, Angelica, 33
Kendall, Ehrengard von Schul-
    enberg, Duchess of, 41, 70,
    79
Kensington Palace, 161
Kent, Duke of, 150
Kent, William, 13
Keppel, Augustus, Hon., 19-20
Kew, 161
Kielmannsegge: see Darlington,
    Countess of
Kingston, 158
Knighton, Sir William, 161, 176
Königsmarck, Count, 41, 56

Lagos, 102
Laguerre, Louis, 33
Law, John, 62
Leicester House, 56, 57, 85
Leiningen, Princess of, 150
Levellers, The, 15
Literature, 35

Liverpool, Earl of, 155, 156, 172,
    174
Locke, John, 33
London, 16-17, 18, 112, 124
    merchants, 103
Lords of the Committees, 59
Louisiana, 113
Luttrell, Col. Henry, 123

Malmesbury, Earl of, 168, 169
Mann, Robert, 78
Manners, 19-20
Marlborough, 1st Duke of, 29,
    38, 40, 45, 47-8
Marlborough, Sarah, Duchess of,
    63
Martinique, 94
Masham, Mrs., 54
Middle Class, the New, 103, 106
    attitude to American War of
    Independence, 129
" Milan Commission ", the, 173
Minden, Battle of, 94, 102
Mississippi Company, 62
Mists's Journal (qu.), 42
Monarchy, Parliamentary, 64 et
    seq.
Monarchy, public contempt for
    the, 148, 152-3, 174
Murray, General, 125

Namier, Sir Lewis (qu.), 127
Napoleon, 155
Nash, John, 163
National Debt, 62-3
National Gallery, 163
Nelson, Horatio, 14
Nepotism, 20, 77-8
Neville, Sylas, Diary of, 116
Newcastle, Duke of, 55, 88, 92,
    98, 102, 105, 124
Newnham, Mother, 16
Newspapers, Opposition, 78, 80,
    104, 105-6
Newton, Sir Isaac, 33, 102

North Briton, 105-6
North, Lord, 99, 102, 118-26, 133
Nottingham, Earl of, 39, 47

O'Connell, Daniel, 157
Oligarchy, 26
Ormonde, Duke of, 40, 46
Owen, Robert, 150
Oxford, Earl of: *see* Harley, Robert

Paine, Thomas, 24
Paley, William, 26
Palladio, Andrea, 33
Pamphleteers, 80
Pares, Richard, *King George III and the Politicians*, 133
Paris, Peace of, 104, 105, 112-13
Parliament, 52-5, 60-1
George III's attitude to, 127
Parliamentary Monarchy, 64 et seq.
Patronage, political, 57
Peel, Sir Robert, 20, 157, 176
Peerage Bill (1719), 60
Pelham, Henry, 92, 93, 94, 102
Perceval, Spencer, 155, 171
Pergami, 171, 172
Pitt, William (the Elder), 14, 30, 54, 73, 86, 90, 91, 93, 98, 100, 102, 104, 107, 108
Pitt, William (the Younger), 135 et seq., 156
Plays, 80
Pope, Alexander, *Essay on Man*, 107
Population, growth of, 18, 30
Portland, Duke of, 133, 134, 139
Pratt, Mr. Justice, 106, 107
Price, Richard, 129
Priestley, Joseph, 22, 129
Prussia, 90, 162

Pulteney, William, 79, 81, 83, 101
Punishments, 16, 17, 19

Quebec, 92, 94, 102

Reform, 21, 26, 27-8, 77, 128-9
Regency, 143, 147 et seq.
Regent's Park, 162
Reynolds, Sir Joshua, 14
Richmond, 161
Richmond, Duke of, 97
Robethon, Jean, 40-1
" Robinocracy ", the, 78
Rockingham, Marquess of, 54, 116, 130
Romilly, Sir Samuel, 22
Rowlandson, Thomas, 14, 152
Royal family, public contempt for the, 148, 151-2, 174
Rutland, Duchess of, 149
Rysbrack, Michael, 33

St. Laurent, Mme., 150
St. Simon, Duc de, 86
Sandwich, Earl of, 125
Sans Souci Palace, Berlin, 162
Scarborough, Earl of, 76
Schönbrunn, 162
Scotland, Union with, 46
Scott, Sir Walter, 165
Sedgwick, Mr. Romney, 96
Seven Years' War, 91-2, 93, 94, 113
Sheffield Plate, 32
Shelburne, Earl of, 132
Sheraton, Thomas, 32
Sheriffmuir, Battle of, 46
Shipbuilding, 29
Shippen, William, 81
Shrewsbury, Duke of, 37-8
Shrewsbury, Duchess of, 43
Sinecures, 20, 27, 77-8, 132
Sinking Fund, 83
Skerrett, Maria, 76

Slavery, 29, 94, 154
Slums, 17
Smallpox, 17
Society, 23
Society for the Reformation of the Manners of the Lower Orders, 21
Somers, Lord, 47
Somerset, Duke of, 38
Sophia, Princess, 151
Sophia, Dorothy, Queen, 41
South American Republics, recognition of the, 156
Spode china, 32
Southill, Beds., 22
South Sea Bubble, 62, 74
South Sea Company, 27, 61
Spain, 29, 83, 87, 89. 90, 126, 155
Spanish Succession, Wars of the, 28, 29
Speculation, financial, 63
Sports, addiction to cruel, 15-16, 21
Stanhope, Earl, 45, 50
Strutt, Jedediah, 129
Stuart, House of, 37, 46
    First Rising, 46
    Second Rising, 90
Stubbs, George, painting by, 14
Suffolk, riots in, 15
Sunderland, Charles, Earl of, 45, 48, 51, 55, 59, 60, 64
Sussex, Duke of, 150, 170
Swift, Dean, 20

Temple, Earl, 105, 133
Tobacco trade, 112
Tories, the, 37, 39
Townshend, Charles, Viscount, 45, 47, 49, 50, 51, 52, 58, 60, 64, 69, 84, 89
Trade, development of, 30, 62, 90, 95, 102
Transportation (convicts), 19, 29

Troke, Margaret, 17
Tunbridge Wells, 32
Turner, J. M. W., 34
Tyburn, 16

Union with Ireland, 145
Union with Scotland, 46
Universities, 25
Utrecht, Treaty of, 45

Vane, Miss, 86

Wales, Frederick, Prince of, 79, 82, 84, 85, 86, 93
Wales, Princess of: see Caroline of Ansbach, or Augusta Princess of Wales, 163
Wallace Art Collection, 163
Walmoden, Countess, 71, 89
Walpole, Horace, 15, 99
Walpole, Sir Robert, 20, 24, 30, 45, 47, 49, 51, 52, 57, 58, 59, 60, 61, 72-94, 156
    personal character, 73-9
    opposition to his policies, 83
War, Georgian inclination for, 14, 90-1
Watt, James, 129
Wealth, 26, 27, 28, 31, 32
    distribution of, 31
Wedgwood, Josiah, 13, 21, 128
    pottery, 32
Wellesley, Marquess, 15
Wellington, Duke of, 155, 156, 157, 160
Wesley, John, 17, 21, 24
West Indies, 94, 104, 110
Wharton, Philip, Duke of, 47
Whigs, the, 37, 46, 47, 52, 60, 64, 124, 129, 150, 154, 159, 171
Whitbread, Samuel, 22
Whitefield, George, 17
Wilberforce, William, 22, 24, 152

Wilkes, John, 15, 105-8, 115, 122-5
Wilkinson, John, 21
William III, 29, 38, 50, 161
Winchester mutinies, 15
Windham, Ashe (qu.), 89
Windham, Col. William (qu.), 63
Windsor Castle, 162, 176
Wolfe, James, 14, 94

Wood, William, 173
Woodforde, James, 25
Worcester porcelain, 32
Wren, Sir Christopher, 33
Wyatt, James, 176
Wyndham, Sir William, 81

York, Duke of, 149

Zoffany, John, 14